# Plagiarism

# Plagiarism

*Why It Happens • How to Prevent It*

Barry Gilmore

HEINEMANN
Portsmouth, NH

**Heinemann**
361 Hanover Street
Portsmouth, NH 03801–3912
www.heinemann.com

*Offices and agents throughout the world*

**Library of Congress Cataloging-in-Publication Data**
Gilmore, Barry.
    Plagiarism : why it happens how to prevent it / Barry Gilmore.
        p.  cm.
    Includes bibliographical references.
    ISBN-13: 978-0-325-02250-5
    ISBN-10: 0-325-02250-X
    1. Plagiarism.   2. Student ethics—Study and teaching.   I. Title.
PN167.G47  2008
371.5'8—dc22                                            2008020812

*Editor:* Lisa Luedeke
*Production editor:* Sonja S. Chapman
*Cover design:* Night & Day Design
*Compositor:* Kim Arney
*Manufacturing:* Steve Bernier

Printed in the United States of America on acid-free paper
12  11   10   09   08    VP   1   2   3   4   5

# Contents

# Acknowledgments

As I note in the text of this book, after suffering through innumerable surveys, emails, and interviews, the students and faculty with whom I work at Lausanne Collegiate School have gotten pretty tired of talking about plagiarism. I'm indebted to the whole school community, as well as to the students at Martin Luther King Magnet School in Nashville, Tennessee, for sharing their thoughts and experiences; I couldn't hope for better models of good practice than these two schools. A few of my colleagues deserve particular mention, beginning with an expert teacher and editor (and my mother), Dr. Sue Gilmore, and also including, in no particular order, Brenda Robinette, Ginger Reese, Josh Clark, Dana Fountain, Dr. Thomas New, Jamie Gibson, Bill Brown, and Dr. David Perry. As always, I'm grateful to Lisa Luedeke and Sonja Chapman at Heinemann for their encouragement and care. Finally, I am thankful beyond words to my wife, Susanna, and to my daughters Katy and Zoe, who may have begun life as cut-and-paste compilations but have become true originals.

## TOP TEN: Student Tips for Avoiding Plagiarism

1. *Know the definition of plagiarism at your school.* Check with instructors to determine whether collaboration is permitted and what they expect of your bibliography. Remember that *all* ideas and words must be cited.

2. *Take good notes.* Develop strategies such as note cards or spreadsheet files that will help you keep track of sources, authors, URLs, and other important information as you work.

3. *Paraphrase carefully.* Try not to use more than one or two important words from the original source when you paraphrase material (and remember to cite that source even if your material isn't in quotation marks).

4. *Learn to attribute correctly.* Ask teachers what citation format they prefer and learn the basics. For more difficult citations, find a web page or book that will guide you.

5. *Leave plenty of time.* Don't get caught behind a deadline—most plagiarism occurs when students feel desperate or rushed.

6. *Make sure you understand the assignment.* Ask questions in advance that will help you avoid the feeling of being "lost" or overwhelmed.

7. *Research wisely.* Use your research skills for more than a quick web search—learn how to use search engines and the library to find the best possible sources for your projects.

8. *Make your bibliography as you work.* Type your bibliography as you find sources rather than waiting until the final draft of your paper—there are many websites that can help you format a bibliography quickly and easily.

9. *Double-check your papers.* Use a search engine or free plagiarism detection software to check your own papers before you hand them in.

10. *Make the assignment personal.* Try to make assignments important to you. Where possible, tweak topics or arguments to put your own spin on them. Look for what you can learn from the project, not just for the grade you'll receive at the end.

# 1 Introduction

## Taking the Plague Out of Plagiarism

Consider this: In 1892, when she was twelve years old, Helen Keller (yes, *that* Helen Keller) was accused of plagiarism. The work in question was a story titled "The Frost King," substantial portions of which, it turns out, were copied from a story by nineteenth-century author Margaret T. Canby titled "The Frost Fairies."

In her autobiography, Keller admits to borrowing from another's work:

> At that time I eagerly absorbed everything I read without a thought of authorship, and even now I cannot be quite sure of the boundary line between my ideas and those I find in books . . . But the fact remains that Miss Canby's story was read to me once, and that long after I had forgotten it, it came back to me so naturally that I never suspected that it was the child of another mind. (1952, 63)

The accusation and subsequent inquisition of Keller by her teachers, along with the realization that she had, in fact, unwittingly plagiarized a story by another writer, shook Keller. She avoided ever writing fiction again and, if we can believe her assertions of innocence, turned to autobiography partly as a way to prove to herself as well as to others her own authorship.

Flash-forward more than a century, to 2006: Keller's story became a hot topic once more, this time for its usefulness as a comparison with the case of a Harvard sophomore, Kaavya Viswanathan, who was accused of plagiarizing material from two young adult novels by Megan McCafferty. Take, for instance, the *New York Times* article focusing on the young author:

> Under scrutiny, [she] suddenly recalled adoring Ms. McCafferty's books and claimed to have unconsciously channeled them. Given that, her critics charged, she was being treated better than other fabulists of late. . . . But what if she had been deaf and blind? (Zeller 2006)

## YOU NEED TO KNOW: Understanding and Defining the Term *Plagiarism*

Many students think of *plagiarism* only as copying an entire essay and handing it in as one's own, when in fact the term refers to appropriating any material—ideas, writings, images, or portions of those—and claiming to be the original creator.

The word itself is interesting; its most immediate root is the Latin word *plagiarius*, meaning "kidnapper," but that word in turn comes from the older Latin word *plagus*, "net." The metaphors here might resonate with students. What does it mean to kidnap someone's ideas? How does the image of tossing a net over an object to capture it translate to capturing ideas from today's online Net?

It's also worth considering that plagiarism, which applies to questions of authorship, is slightly different from—though related to—forgery (which involves questions of authenticity), copyright infringement (which deals with legal ownership), and the broad label cheating (which implies purposeful deception of any type).

It may seem like splitting hairs to worry too much about definitions—we all know what it means to plagiarize, right? Perhaps as teachers we do, but parents, administrators, students, and the broader community may look for, and find, loopholes. Take the example of an eighth-grade teacher whose students turned in work copied verbatim from an encyclopedia, as is related in an excerpt from *Preventing Cheating and Plagiarism*:

> [The teacher] said they had plagiarized. Some of the kids' parents appealed to the school's Headmistress. Overruling the teacher, she decreed such copying was not plagiarism—at least not when done by 8th graders. (Clabaugh and Rozycki 2003)

It's worthwhile, therefore, to construct a written definition of plagiarism to work with, preferably for your entire school community, but at least in your own course syllabus. That's not a guarantee that no one will challenge your definition, but, as Clabaugh and Rozycki suggest, "A dictionary definition is better than mere assertion. . . . Dealing effectively with plagiarism requires definitional clarity."

It's a good question, perhaps, but one that doesn't eclipse all other questions. What, for instance, if the Harvard student had been twelve, like Keller, instead of nineteen? What if Keller had just signed a half-million-dollar book deal instead of just showing her story to a teacher? What if Keller had been able to check her work easily and quickly with a Google search or by running it through a paper-checking site like Turnitin.com? And, too, this one: What if Keller's error had become fodder for every blog and website that chose to take up the issue and the fallout had been so thick and sudden she'd been assured of never getting published again?

When we think about plagiarism, in other words, are we asking all of the right questions?

## The Nature of the Problem

Plagiarism is easier than ever to commit, is trickier than ever to judge, and resists facile response by educators as much in the twenty-first century as it did in the nineteenth. The very tools available to students have changed the entire landscape of research and writing; if, as a teacher, you're anything like me, you've tried to keep up with that shifting landscape, but it's overwhelming. Just before writing this sentence, for instance, I ran a quick Google search for references to Margaret T. Canby (the author from whom Keller copied her work). Google spit back more than eighty-six thousand results, but the first ten displayed—one screen—simply redirected me back to Keller's autobiography. Rather than paging through all eighty-six thousand sites, I pretty quickly decided just to give up my search—turns out I'm just not quite interested enough in Margaret T. Canby to browse through all of those Google pages.

On the other hand, a quick search for "Helen Keller papers" brought an instant reward: site after site of free term papers, essays, and research projects on the work of Helen Keller. The names of these "paper mills" sometimes say a lot about the content of the sites and their intended subscribers; there's Echeat.com, Fratfiles.com, Schoolsucks.com. Many of the sites will even write custom essays for students for about the same amount many teachers spend at Starbucks on their way to school, and to make matters worse, students can even buy papers that are less than excellent; you can pay good money for a C+ paper that will fool your teacher *just* enough.

So there, in a nutshell, is the terrain of research these days: it's far, far easier for many students to find a prewritten paper on a topic than to do research on one. Especially solid, academic research. To do that, one might even have to—gasp—visit a real library. With *books*.

That's not to say the Internet isn't a wonderful tool—it is. I accessed the *New York Times* article I cited earlier online. I gathered a lot of information for this book online. I'm not arguing a Luddite's position or that we should force students never to use online resources. Just the contrary: In a world where students not only will but *should* take advantage of the immense resources available to them, it's more important than ever that teachers guide them toward a strong sense of digital literacy and academic integrity. We shouldn't simply expect students not to cheat; we need to give them the tools to avoid cheating.

To compile those tools, we need to understand our students and *why* they cheat. We need to understand the academic culture in which they operate and the ways in which some teachers enable or even encourage plagiarism. And we need to understand that plagiarism and cheating may not always be quite synonymous, or at least that intent and response at the individual level matter. Notice, for instance, how Helen Keller felt when she discovered that she had appropriated another's words:

> The two stories were so much alike in thought and language that it was evident Miss Canby's story had been read to me, and that mine was—a plagiarism. It was difficult to make me understand this; but when I did understand I was astonished and grieved. No child ever drank deeper of the cup of bitterness than I did. I had disgraced myself; I had brought suspicion upon those I loved best. . . . As I lay in my bed that night, I wept as I hope few children have wept. I felt so cold, I imagined I should die before morning, and the thought comforted me. I think if this sorrow had come to me when I was older, it would have broken my spirit beyond repairing. (1952, 64)

And here, by way of contrast, is how Senator Joseph Biden, in the midst of a presidential campaign in 1987, responded to reports that he had plagiarized an article in law school:

> "I was wrong, but I was not malevolent in any way," Mr. Biden said. "I did not intentionally move to mislead anybody. And I didn't. To this day I didn't." (Dionne 1987)

I'm not sure that any student cheats out of malevolence, but I take the point. When I first read about Biden's plagiarism, I was appalled, and the idea of plagiarism without "malevolence" sounded to me like a dog-ate-my-homework bit (or, these days, a damaged hard drive). But later I wondered if, in fact, his statement that he "had simply misunderstood the need to cite sources carefully" might hold some validity. Had anyone ever taught him how to cite sources? Had he simply had a phrase like "academic integrity" tossed at him in a student handbook, or had it been explained? Were the pressures of his academic system so great that he felt compelled to plagiarize, perhaps because he felt his peers were doing it already? Without making excuses, is there, I wondered, room for understanding, even sympathy?

## What's Our Real Concern?

The premise of this book is not that plagiarism is always inevitable nor always excusable, but that once a teacher is reduced to the role of source detective, he has already lost an educational battle. Wouldn't most detectives, after all, prefer stopping the crime in the first place to merely finding and punishing offenders? This is a book, then, about school and classroom culture, about assignment making, and about educating students in areas such as research, process writing, and attribution. It also covers detection and response, because educators need tools and policies to handle the crime when it does occur, but I wish always to place detection—and consequence—within the larger context of education.

> **Voices from the Classroom**
>
> I'm always afraid that I'll accidentally forget to cite something or have my quotation marks in the wrong place—not that any severe punishment will be exercised at my school, but that when I go to a college next year, it may not be seen as the mistake that it is because the teachers there won't know me yet and may put the honest me in a pool of those "cheating kids."
>
> —*Laura, age seventeen*

Or, to use another comparison, think of teachers as doctors. Don't compare plagiarism itself to a disease, no matter how many times authors like me cleverly pull *plague* out of the word; the metaphor won't necessarily stand up. And for goodness' sake don't start comparing the average salaries of doctors to those of teachers. But imagine the aspects of illness doctors concern themselves with: prevention, symptoms, diagnosis, prognosis, treatment. If we follow this model, we don't want to be, as educators, the equivalent of the highly trained and specialized surgeon who steps in at the last moment to orchestrate and carry out an organ transplant (we may want to be treated as that sort of specialist in other areas of our profession, but not this one). If we find ourselves in that role, all that's left us is a drastic response: cut out the illness, fix what we can. To encourage academic integrity, teachers should rather be the insightful and deductive general practitioner, the one who helps patients find the right mix of diet and exercise and testing to forestall the downward spiral into poor health in the first place, but who also catches the signs of illness and knows how to point patients in the direction of a cure. Or perhaps we must be both diagnostician and surgeon at times, but if so, we must at least balance the one job against the other.

**Voices from the Classroom**

Has plagiarism gotten worse? I've been teaching for forty years, and I really think problems with plagiarism have gotten better. Students aren't having to cite from books; they can go on the Internet and it's no big deal to put quotes around it. If all I have to do is put quotation marks around it, I don't mind hitting another key on the computer. But if you were never told it was wrong, if it was never emphasized in class, or it was never said to you, "I'm going to turn you in to Turnitin.com," and you thought you could sneak it past me, you probably would. But now, with all these checks, what's the sense?

—*Ninth-grade teacher*

Prevention, symptoms, diagnosis, prognosis, treatment. That's the ideal, but you may feel, as a classroom practitioner, that you're constantly doing triage—stemming the worst wounds in a constant panic just to stop the bleeding. We all feel that way, sometimes, about writing, about reading, and most certainly about plagiarism and cheating, if for no other reason than when we catch the worst offenders, the crime has already been committed—we enter at the tail end of the story and have no options left except simple response or even punishment. We feel betrayed; we take it personally, as if the criminal had stolen from us, as if the patient's illness were a personal affront, as if the student had violated our trust out of, well, malevolence.

And in response, we vow to ourselves to become better watchdogs, to make sure it doesn't happen again. Or, worse, we deal with one student and then go right back about our business, hoping it won't happen again—we stemmed the bleeding, after all, and the rest is out of our hands.

The rest is not out of our hands.

If any of the above symptoms of the betrayed teacher sound familiar, know that you aren't alone. I use the first-person plural because I've been as rocked by cases of plagiarism and as dismayed at my role, before and after, as any other classroom teacher. I recall the sinking feeling in my gut when I realized that a student I really liked—one who had asked me for a recommendation to the Naval Academy—had copied a friend's work almost word for word. I remember the time I trusted a young woman to make up an essay test at home rather than in her study hall only to discover she'd saved her sister's work from two years before and turned it in as her own. And if plagiarism isn't always malevolent, I've at times turned malevolent in response to plagiarism, Googling sentences with a certain wild-eyed malice that I usually reserve for people who talk on their cell phones during movies or student teachers who leave the photocopier with a paper jam when I'm late to class and trying to run off a quiz.

Take a deep breath as you read this book. Teaching *is* personal; I don't blame anyone who takes the callous or just plain thoughtless actions of students to heart. Revenge isn't the answer, though, even if it sometimes feels good in the short term, nor are other short-term responses to bad teaching days (I, too, have been known to gobble down the last three doughnuts in the teachers lounge between classes in some misplaced attempt at self-consolation—who hasn't?). If you're stuck responding to a case of plagiarism, be prepared to do so. If treatment is needed, give it. But (and I try to write this without moralizing) don't forget the steps that lead to that end or the benefits of planning, of careful design of lessons, and, ultimately, of education. Someday, when one of your students runs for president, perhaps he—or, better, she—will tell the press that yes, she did attribute sources incorrectly, but fortunately there was a fine teacher who, instead of sending her straight to the gallows, showed her the problem and helped her correct it before it kept her from writing—or running—at all.

> ### Voices from the Classroom
>
> I think there is more pressure to get into college than there used to be—before, getting a bachelor's was a big thing; now everybody getting into some level of professionalism gets a bachelor's degree. There's a lot of pressure, therefore, from parents to get into a better college, and they put a lot of pressure on themselves, too, I think. It's more about the grades you make in their minds than what you've learned or whether you're doing the right thing.
>
> —*Guidance counselor*

## What You'll Find in This Book

Every teacher has a story or ten about plagiarism. On the surface, these stories seem to run along similar lines—kids get behind, get careless, and get caught. Motivations, reactions, and responses, however, differ from case to case.

If we're going to talk about plagiarism, we need to remember that when it happens, it happens because of an individual student and, sometimes, an individual teacher, and their stories matter, even if overarching policies or ideals affect them similarly. Throughout this book, you'll find sidebars containing some of these actual stories by teachers and students—stories that, I believe, throw into sharp relief the difficulty of a one-size-fits-all approach to educating about plagiarism and suggest that ordinary classroom teachers constantly struggle to figure out how to best handle these difficult situations.

And since this book is for ordinary classroom teachers who are constantly developing their own stories about arbitration and response, I've organized it with the teacher in mind. Although I believe strongly in the need for education and prevention, I also know from bitter experience that when a case of student plagiarism strikes, it strikes hard. So I've arranged the chapters for a teacher who may have a paper of questionable authenticity sitting on his desk *right now*—who may be deeply concerned about the student, about being fair, about the perceptions of the rest of the class, about dealing with parents and administrators, and just about getting it all right.

First, then, for that teacher, comes detection. Is the paper plagiarized and, if so, from what source? Who else knows and how do you prove it? Those questions, along with strategies for guiding students away from various types of plagiarism, are covered in the next chapter, Chapter 2.

After detection comes response, but choosing between alternatives for response also requires us to practice another type of detection, one that's often more challenging than merely uncovering the crime. Chapter 3, therefore, discusses the importance of uncovering motives and offering students a chance to explain their actions and, through explanation, to reflect. Finding out *why* a student plagiarized is a key not just to helping that student learn but also to restructuring assignments, policies, and perhaps even the culture of a classroom or school.

Chapter 4 covers the options for immediate, short-term response once a teacher *does* discover a case of plagiarism, and after motives have been considered. Such response includes, but isn't limited, consequences and possibilities for correction. This chapter also considers the roles of teachers, administrators, and parents in cases of academic dishonesty.

Next comes long-term response. Though I'd love to emphasize the importance of applying foresight and preventing plagiarism by placing it first, the truth is that most teachers deal with a few actual students and situations first, then revisit the way they structure assignments and educate students on the front end. So Chapters 5 and 6 deal with long-term response in the classroom, with teaching citation rules and designing assignments and assessments, and Chapter 7 addresses issues that affect entire schools such as honor codes, school culture, and overarching policies.

In addition, you'll find other kinds of supplementary information scattered throughout the chapters of this book. The voices of researchers and educational journalists often summarize ideas and approaches well enough that I wish to add their thoughts to my own. I've also included  statistics and graphs that illustrate the current educational climate regarding plagiarism. And, too, I included material that reflects my own school and classroom.

> ### Voices from the Classroom
>
> No one is going to rat you out for cheating because everyone's done it. If we all started turning each other in, we'd be hypocrites stabbing each other in the back. It would just be a mess. The few that have never cheated aren't going to say anything either, because the odds are so incredibly turned against them.
>
> —*Aaron, age fifteen*

But the heart and soul of any book that is useful for classroom teachers are lesson plans, practical strategies, and teaching ideas that help us operate daily. In each chapter, you'll find just such methods presented as succinctly as possible, often using bullet points or numbered lists for your own ease. These strategies can be adopted and transformed as necessary for your classroom, the grade level you teach, or your distinct student population—use them as you need to (and no, you don't even need to provide an MLA citation when you do).

## Moving Forward

It's easy to feel discouraged when you read about plagiarism; the statistics are disheartening, especially for those of us who actually *enjoy* writing, and articles on the subject almost always begin with the most dire and frightening statistics available.

But plagiarists aren't always copying the work of others because they hate writing or because they're lazy. Sometimes they fit both these categories, sure, but not always. And whether the crime is intentional or inadvertent, egregious or subtle, the students we deal with are, generally, adolescents. The mixture of emotions that comes with an accusation of plagiarism—guilt, embarrassment, anger, defensiveness—shouldn't allow students to escape consequences, but it places more responsibility on teachers at all levels to be deliberate, calm, and rational in dealing with such cases.

Again, consider the twelve-year-old Helen Keller:

> I never knew even the names of the members of the "court" who did not speak to me. I was too excited to notice anything, too frightened to ask questions. Indeed, I could scarcely think what I was saying, or what was being said to me. (1952, 69)

A nineteen-year-old is, perhaps, a different matter. Viswanathan appeared on the *Today* show shortly after the media identified more than forty passages of nearly identical syntax and diction—right down to the use of italics—between her book and others; in that interview, she still claimed ignorance and announced plans to reissue the book with revisions and an added preface (no publisher took her up on it). Yet that's not to say that a high school senior, for instance, might not feel the guilt and despair Keller describes. It's not to say that students always have the foresight not to compound one lie with another or not simply to shut down when confronted. And, as with almost every story, there was more to Viswanathan's than initially met the eye. Her book, it turned out, had been packaged by an entertainment company that redirected the plot, characterizations, and overall ideas of the novel from a few sample chapters. There were other pressures in play, too; reporter Mark Patinkin

### Voices from the Classroom

Plagiarism? I'd define it as an easy A if you don't get caught, and an easy F if you do.

—*Anton, age fourteen*

(2006) noted, "It appears another reason this happened is that Kaavya was pushed by adults who seemed even more obsessed than she was with her success." Were her actions excusable? No. But if I were her teacher, I'd want to know the whole story.

I hope as you read this book, you'll look for strategies both to deal with plagiarism and to avoid it in the first place, but I also hope you'll take the time to define your own attitude toward such cases. Policy is important; demeanor is, too. Plagiarism *isn't* a disease, even if it's convenient to discuss it as one and even if it feels pandemic in our society; plagiarism is a mistake, one that we, at the best, can help students avoid, and at the worst, can still use as an opportunity for further education and learning.

## Works Cited

Clabaugh, Gary K., and Edward G. Rozycki. 2003. "Defining Plagiarism." In *Preventing Cheating and Plagiarism*, 2d ed. Oreland, PA: NewFoundations. www.newfoundations.com/PREVPLAGWEB/DefiningPlagiarism.html (accessed Feb. 19, 2008).

Dionne, E. J. Jr. 1987. "Biden Admits Plagiarism in School but Says It Was Not 'Malevolent.'" *New York Times*, Sept. 18. http://query.nytimes.com/gst/fullpage.html?res=9B0DE3DB143FF93BA2575AC0A961948260 (accessed Feb. 8, 2008).

Keller, Helen. 1952. *The Story of My Life*. Garden City, NY: Doubleday.

Patinkin, Mark. 2006. "How Kaavya Viswanathan Got Herself Packaged." *Providence Journal*, Sept. 5. www.shns.com/shns/g_index2 .cfm?action=detail&pk=PATINKIN-05-09-06 (accessed Feb. 8, 2008).

Zeller, Tom Jr. 2006. "In Internet Age, Writers Face Frontier Justice." *New York Times*, May 1. www.nytimes.com/2006/05/01/business/media/01link.html?_ r=1&th&emc=th&oref=slogin (accessed Feb. 8, 2008).

# 2 Copies (and Robberies)

## How Students Plagiarize

It's five o'clock, school's been out for two hours, and thirty or forty papers into a stack of essays on *The Adventures of Huckleberry Finn*, I come across this paragraph:

> A father is suppose to wish the best for his children, but Pap seems to dislike the idea that his on is getting an education, becoming better that who he was. The new judge in town returns Huck to Pap because he privileges Pap's "rights" over Huck's welfare—just as slaves, because they were considered property, were regularly returned to their legal owners, no matter how badly these owners abused them. "You think you're better'n your father, now, don't you, because he can't?" These examples teach us something about Huck and about society. Huck is at the center of countless failures and breakdowns in the society around him, yet he maintains his characteristic resilience.[*]

My heart sinks. I'm tired, I'm just about ready to go home, and now I have what I strongly suspect is a case of plagiarism on my hands. While the typos in the first sentence and the odd use of *privileges* as a verb seem realistic enough, the student who wrote this paragraph, based on my previous experience, is about as likely to use a phrase like "characteristic resilience" as he is to write in Sumerian. The historical commentary raises my eyebrows, too. I don't relish the thought of confronting him about it, but I like even less the idea that he'll get away with it and, therefore, do it again, and maybe set an example for others.

---

[*] Confession time: While the scenario I'm describing is real, I substituted the original offending paragraph with one I cobbled together myself from online sources. It contains plagiarized material that I *haven't* cited here just to make the point; all sources are identified and cited later in this chapter and are included in the Works Cited list on page 34.

## TOP TEN: Signs That a Paper Includes Plagiarism

1. *Diction and phrasing.* The paper includes some words, phrases, or sentences that are more sophisticated than the rest of the student's work. Awkward transitions leading to more sophisticated prose are sometimes a sign, as well.

2. *Formatting inconsistencies.* It's amazing how often students won't think to change the font of a cut-and-paste job or have trouble converting html line spacing into the format of a Word document.

3. *Types of sources.* If the sources are obscure, don't easily come up in a quick online search, aren't available in the school library, or have titles that don't obviously have anything to do with the topic (even if the source itself is on topic), it might be worth checking the bibliography more carefully.

4. *Plot summary.* Although students summarize the plot in analytical papers all the time, a good deal of plot summary in a paper can also be a sign of a cut-and-paste job from an online study guide.

5. *An inability to discuss the thesis or process orally.* Instead of starting with accusations, consider this question: "That was a really interesting source to include—how did you find it?" Annotated bibliographies are also a help.

6. *Unusual spelling, including British forms of words.* If the student writes *colour* instead of *color* or *theatre* instead of *theater*, look more closely (Tenbusch 2002).

7. *The paper sounds suspiciously like another paper from the same class.* If you get this feeling, look back through the other essays and do a side-by-side comparison of any that seem closely related.

8. *Inconsistencies in content or argument.* Sometimes students will try to cobble ideas together that loosely relate to the assigned topic or question. Illogical and tangential leaps can be a sign that material was drawn together from other sources.

9. *Quotations with citation.* Watch quoted material from both primary and secondary sources. Watch also for citations that include different line or page numbers from the edition of a source you use in class.

10. *A history of plagiarism, last-minute or late papers, and other behavioral signs.* Cases of plagiarism aren't limited to the best or worst students, but an astute teacher can pick up cues from students that they've plagiarized or, sometimes, that others in the class have plagiarized. It's worth a bit of informal discussion on the day papers are due ("So, who was still writing during lunch today?") to see the reaction of an entire class to talking about the process. Sometimes, such discussions *eliminate* your suspicions—a much better result than you might have hoped for.

A good while later, instead of packing the remaining papers in my bag and heading home, I'm still sitting there thinking about the big picture. How widespread *is* plagiarism in my classes, I wonder? How can I prevent it? Is our school policy effective or ineffective, fair or unfair in dealing with such cases?

Eventually, though, I'm forced to consider the implications of the individual paper in front of me. Before I revise policy or assignments, I'll have to deal with *this* essay. I may have to call the parents, talk to an administrator, and challenge the student. Before I do *that*, I'll need proof, and to gather proof, I'll need some idea of where the paper might have come from. It's not that I enjoy playing the role of source investigator, nor is advice in this area, I hope, the most important part of a discussion about preventing plagiarism, but it's where we all start.

In this chapter, therefore, you'll find information helpful to the teacher-reluctantly-turned-sleuth: types of plagiarism and how to identify a student's sources of plagiarized material.

## Addressing Plagiarism (and Detection) in Class

Why discuss plagiarism and detection with students? Though I've said it already, it's worth repeating here: our goal, as teachers, should be to reach a point where we don't have to play detective in the first place. We want to create an environment in which there's no way for students to plagiarize or, better yet, in which students could plagiarize but don't. Later in this book, you'll find plenty of ideas for modifying writing assignments so that students just plain don't cheat. For now, consider that cheating-free classrooms include transparency and mutual understanding of the roles of teacher and student. That transparency and that understanding extend to methods of detecting plagiarism; students need to know our views of plagiarism and how we might act to detect or prevent it *before* they do it. Here are some other reasons I think it's valuable to engage students in exercises that involve detecting possible plagiarism:

- such exercises give students a feeling of what it's like to be a teacher reading, reviewing, and commenting on others' words;
- the knowledge that a teacher has resources at her disposal may deter students from engaging in plagiarism;
- lessons about detection may provoke honest and thoughtful discussion about the nature of plagiarism and cheating in education;
- involving your entire class in detection exercises, in the best-case scenario, keeps you as the teacher from being solely responsible for playing the role of plagiarism cop and wasting valuable hours checking sources; and
- such lessons may allow students a chance to correct a horrible mistake before it becomes an official, irreversible act of theft.

The dangers of such methods, however, should be emphasized. First of all, the goal of detection exercises is emphatically *not* to pit students against one another or to embarrass plagiarizers in front of their peers, and we must be sensitive to the possibility of such results. In addition, the goal is not to create smarter criminals—frank and open discussion must accompany such lessons so that students don't use their knowledge to find more convincing ways to cheat.

After the description of each type of student plagiarism that follows, therefore, you'll find a section called "Teaching Opportunities" that suggests ways to broach the subject of plagiarism with students. It's my hope that through such activities you'll be able to guide students toward using, not abusing, their knowledge of what plagiarism is and how it most often crops up in classes.

## What's on the Menu? The Types of Plagiarism

I love food, but sometimes even I have trouble sorting out what to eat and what to avoid at a potluck dinner. I often describe the Internet to my students as one big potluck. Nearly everyone in the world has brought a dish to the table. Some are delectable; others resemble the cornflake-topped eggplant casserole your wacky aunt used to produce at every family gathering; still others are practically poisonous or taste like cardboard, no matter how lovely their appearance. The world of published words contains much nutritious and edible cuisine, but it can also be as

## My School, My Classroom

I asked nearly two hundred students in grades 7–12 at my school to tell me—anonymously—which types of plagiarism they had practiced within the last year. Students were allowed more than one answer. The answers, by percentage, appear in the chart below. While these results may not be an accurate reflection of national trends, they do paint an interesting picture of one group of suburban adolescents.

For a similar survey you can use with students at your school, see the *Plagiarism Study Guide* available online at www.heinemann .com/gilmore.

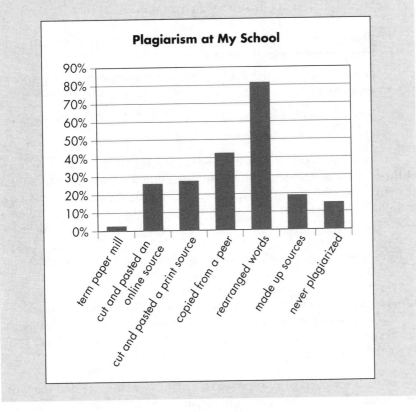

**Plagiarism at My School**

hard to make a decision or to discern the ingredients in the library as it is with the online buffet table.

What I want, I tell my students, is for you to eat, but to eat wisely. Know who made the dish and why. Know who uses only the freshest ingredients and who's likely to leave you with stomach cramps. Know the difference between taste and nutrition and make wise choices that give you both.

When students don't make those wise choices, we need to be able to locate the source of the problem. So here, for your guidance, is a brief menu of bad food, where it comes from, and the signs that a student may have indulged a bit too freely from the potluck choices.

### Ordering In: Term Paper Mills and Cheat Sites

Need a five-page paper in the next twelve hours? Here are some of the perks the website ItchyBrainsCentral (n.d.) can promise you (if you don't believe me, just check it out at www.itchybrainscentral.com):

- papers that are 100 percent custom written by "professional and experienced academic writers"
- editing of a paper the site has sold you if it doesn't meet your exact requirements ("No Questions Asked and it's Free!")
- the sources used in the paper, by email or fax, for an additional fee

The service, of course, is a bit more expensive than the average, run-of-the-mill cheat site that will instantly sell you a prewritten paper for a few bucks, but the guarantee of *originality* is worth it, right? The service is so valuable, in fact, that there's a whole page of the site devoted to doctoral candidates:

> This is not the time to think; this is the time to take action! And, we are here to help take some of that burden from your shoulders so that you can remain sane and continue with life and your studies—and eventually graduate. . . . This is not a warehouse with completed documents that can be downloaded at your choosing. We have warm-blooded, live writers, well prepared to work with you right to the end of the dissertation.

My favorite part of this message is, by far, the assurance that the writers employed by the company are warm-blooded and not, for instance, the reptilian creatures one might mistakenly assume them to be.

Cheat sites have multiplied alarmingly over the last several years. The Kimbel Library at Coastal Carolina University, for instance, began tracking free essay sites in 1999. There were then 36 such sites in its list; by late 2006 there were more than 250 (including ItchyBrainsCentral) (Bates and Fain 2006). Almost all of these sites include disclaimers that their products are not meant to be turned in by students as original work. The itchy brains, in fact, devote an entire five (badly written) paragraphs to answering the question "Plagiarism?" Here's a sample of their argument:

> It would be silly to believe that the student's work is not plagiarized ONLY because s/he performed 100 percent of the work. The reason for that is simple—today, it is not possible to separate "allowed" from "not allowed" materials that are used during the process of doing homework. . . . Students paying for custom essay writing services assess that their cost to make money to pay is lesser than their cost to do the writing on their own. Thus, it is education at work.

## Example of a Ninth-Grader's Plagiarism

A ninth-grade student at my school turned in the following two sentences for an honors-level biology assignment:

> Sickle-cell anemia, a blood disorder caused when red blood cells assume an abnormal shape like a sickle, is caused by cells that don't last as long as round cells and are deprived of oxygen. The painful disease causes organ damage, period attacks, and is chronic.

When I typed "sickle-cell anemia" into a search engine, I immediately retrieved the following passages. Note that the student's writing does not *quite* summarize either passage accurately.

### Internet Sample 1

Sickle-cell disease is a blood disorder characterised by red blood cells that assume an abnormal, rigid, sickle shape. Sickling decreases the cells' flexibility and results in their restricted movement through blood vessels, depriving downstream tissues of oxygen. The disease is chronic and lifelong: individuals are most often well, but their lives are punctuated by periodic painful attacks. (Wikipedia contributors 2008)

### Internet Sample 2

Sickle cell anemia is a disease in which your body produces abnormally shaped red blood cells. The cells are shaped like a crescent or sickle. They don't last as long as normal, round red blood cells, which leads to anemia. The sickle cells also get stuck in blood vessels, blocking blood flow. This can cause pain and organ damage. (U.S. National Library of Medicine 2008)

The itchy brains claim the moral high ground, or at least some equivalency, while others simply warn the user that plagiarism could have serious consequences, but the simple truth is that such sites exist only because there are students who are willing to pay for essays rather than write them on their own. They're businesses, and they've made plagiarism into an industry. You can now order in your eighth-grade book report or master's thesis the way you'd have a pizza delivered to your house—any toppings, any sides. There are even sites that let you *sell* your work to the highest bidder, no matter whether you're a doctoral candidate or a freshman with a D–average out to make a quick buck.

The complete downloading of papers from online sources is less common than some of the other practices I describe in this chapter. It's still common enough, however, to constitute a growing concern for educators. One instructor told me that the problem had driven him to conduct all student writing assignments in class, but he wasn't particularly happy

## YOU NEED TO KNOW: How Widespread Is the Problem?

The following statistics represent the percentage of students who

- have engaged in cut-and-paste plagiarism: 40 percent (Muha 2003)

- say internet plagiarism "is not a serious issue": 77 percent (Campbell 2007)

- have submitted a paper taken, in large part or in whole, from a term paper mill or website: 15 percent (iParadigms 2007)

- have copied a few sentences from a website without citing the source: 52 percent (iParadigms 2007)

- consider copying a few sentences without citation a "serious" offense: 35 percent (College Administration Publications n.d.)

Try using these statistics—and others in this book—as the basis for a survey of your own classes. Compare the results and ask students to discuss with you why the figures for your school are higher or lower than national averages. What does this say about the culture of your school and classroom? How do your students feel about the results? Do they have any suggestions for change?

with the solution, as it robbed those students of the meditative, process-driven time crucial to developing writing habits and skills. Other teachers routinely use the source-checking site Turnitin.com (more on that a little later) or simply rely on Google to help them catch the most flagrant violations. "I think of it like speeding tickets," one colleague told me. "Lots of people speed, and not everyone gets caught, but knowing that *some* people get caught keeps you from speeding too badly and makes sure that you know it when you're breaking the limit. I can't catch everyone with Google, but I can catch enough to scare the rest."

## Teaching Opportunities

What you don't want to try is searching every conceivable cheat site to find the particular paper you're looking for, any more than you'd want to call every Chinese restaurant in the phone book to see which one delivered the nauseating sweet and sour chicken to the student who added it to the buffet. Instead, noticing the signs is the key. If you identify the right sentence or phrase, tools like search engines and detection software become far more handy. But even without the online tools, letting students know you're aware of such sites and discussing them with a class can go a long way toward steering students in a different direction. Let's look at both the nature of electronic detection and how discussion can help.

According to its website, Turnitin.com, the most popular online service for detecting electronic plagiarism, maintains a database of more than forty million student papers and includes more than twelve billion web pages and over ten thousand major news sources when it conducts a search for plagiarism in a student paper (iParadigms 2007). Work can be submitted by a teacher directly or by a student in the teacher's class; either way, the service quickly returns a color-coded version of the paper with potentially plagiarized passages marked and annotated.

Does it work? It seems to. A pie chart on the website suggests that 30 percent of the papers it handles contain some form of plagiarism (you can read about the results of my own experiment with the service in the sidebar titled "How Good Are Electronic Detection Services?" on page 27). Are there concerns? One issue that's been raised in the media is a question of author ownership, but according to the company's founder, John Barrie, "the papers always remain the property of the author" (NPR 2006). A more pressing question, perhaps, is whether such services destroy the trust-based relationship that many teachers work hard to build. Through requiring students to use the service is the message you send that everyone is guilty until proven innocent? Does the service stop plagiarists at the expense of a lesson about academic integrity?

Researcher Donald McCabe raised this point in the same interview with John Barrie mentioned earlier:

> I believe some faculty members are using Turnitin.com more creatively than others. And that is, faculty members who ask their students to submit their papers to Turnitin.com, and the report goes back to the student.

What McCabe suggests, in effect, is using such services to have students teach themselves what's acceptable and what isn't. Obviously, a paper taken wholesale from the Internet will show up with every line marked, and one written by a custom writing service might not show up at all. For the in-between cases, those described at length in the rest of this chapter, such self-monitoring might go a long way toward helping students figure out when they have or haven't done a good job of attributing their source material.

If you have access to a computer in your classroom you can also encourage students to use a search engine for similar self-monitoring. Try having students work in pairs—each partner should type random phrases from the other's written work into a browser and search for them. No report needs to be made to the teacher, here; the point is not to punish students for plagiarism but to give them a chance to see (and to think about) potentially problematic passages from their essays (remind them to check their bibliographies as well as in-text citations for accuracy during this exercise). Even partners who catch no obvious instances of plagiarism in one another's papers will come away with a better idea of how similar their language and ideas are to material available on the Web and, ideally, will discuss *with one another* the dangers of copying work and failing to cite properly.

### Sure, I Cooked That: Peer Copying

Term paper mills aren't the only way students obtain full essays. If using a cheat site is the equivalent of ordering food from a restaurant and passing it off as your own creation, copying a friend's paper word for word is like switching the nameplates on the buffet table to take credit for what isn't yours. It happens fairly often—students are convinced teachers don't *really* read the papers (and sometimes, they're probably correct) and therefore the assignment constitutes busywork, so why not take a shortcut?

With peer copying, there's also a social element added to the mix. What do you do if your best friend in tenth grade asks to copy your paper? What if you're a freshman and a junior asks? Not every student is prepared for such a situation.

This kind of cheating, by the way, leaves the burden of detection squarely on the teacher, unless that teacher happens to use a service such as Turnitin.com, which will flag papers that are similar to other student papers as well as to online sources. The trouble? Sometimes it's clear that one student copied another, but impossible to tell who copied first. My own most nettlesome experiences with talking to students about plagiarism have involved work copied from peers. And, too, not all teachers are willing to bother with an electronic service for relatively minor assignments such as homework or vocabulary sentences.

## Teaching Opportunities

It's my own belief that most middle and high school students follow rules better when the impetus to do so comes not just from the potential consequences but also from consistent reinforcement in several areas: students need role models, they need to discuss issues and rules and understand *why* the rules exist in the first place, they need chances to self-correct, they need to see that enforcement is consistent and fair. When I have students share their writing, then, it's never meant simply to catch plagiarists, but if the by-product is increased self-vigilance, that's fine. With that in mind:

- Have students trade rough drafts in class. If you wish, have each student underline his thesis or topic sentence before handing a partner the paper, or have the partners do this with the papers they receive. Then, instruct all students to write a thesis or topic sentence from the paper they received on the board or on sheets of big paper posted around the room. There are multiple benefits here, not least of which is the chance to discuss the nature of the central sentence and

### Voices from the Classroom

My last experience with plagiarism was complex. Two students turned in papers that shared about 40 percent of the same material. The phrasings were identical, but their placement in the papers differed. They also included the same irrelevant material that didn't really have anything to do with the topic. One of the papers was pretty good, otherwise. The other was pretty lousy. Finally, there were a few sentences lifted word for word from the textbook, but just two or so.

I did a Web search or five. I typed the repeating paragraphs into Turnitin.com. I couldn't find any external source. So, I called each student in and spoke to them independently. The first claimed that they studied together and put together notes, and then he wrote his paper from notes which must have been the same as his peer's notes. He couldn't produce said notes. The second said much the same thing, but also said that he wrote his paper first and let his friend look at it. When confronted, the first said he had never seen his friend's paper. Later, he came back and said that he had written his paper first, and then had gone to bed at about 4 A.M. with his friend still not having written.

In the letter I wrote to the students, I included this: "I cannot prove what, exactly, happened. . . . In the end, I am left only with the two papers and their shared sentences. Both of you will receive an F, a 59 percent, on the papers." What else could I do?

—*College professor*

idea in each paper. If the same sentence comes up twice, you can point it out without accusing or moralizing. If a sentence with particularly sophisticated syntax comes up, you can point that out, too, not simply by praising it but by saying, for instance, "That sentence sounds very professional; I wonder how the rest of the piece sounds." The key here is then to give students some time in class or at home to revise before turning the piece in (revision is good classroom practice, anyway).

- Provide an audience for written assignments (also good classroom practice, anyway). Have students peer edit; post their work on an internal website or on a bulletin board; ask students to have their parents sign the assignment stating merely that they've read it. When a student knows that more eyes will regularly cross the page, she not only is less likely to regard a piece of writing as busywork that begs to be copied but will also feel better about the product she produces in general.

- Some research has suggested that signing an honor pledge decreases the likelihood that students will plagiarize (McCabe and Trevino 1993). You'll find a more detailed discussion of honor codes and pledges in Chapter 7 of this book, but for the moment, consider that a simple honor pledge on all papers, no matter how minor the assignment, forces both the one copying and the one allowing the copying to make a statement on record (pledges commonly use a simple statement that the student has "neither given nor received help on this assignment"); because of this dual assignment of responsibility, an honor pledge might be particularly useful in situations of peer copying.

- In my own classroom, I frequently instruct students to complete individualized assignments—they're more interesting to me to read and more interesting to them to write. This is true of essays, but also of minor homework assignments. Each student, for

## Voices from the Classroom

Plagiarism comes hand in hand with procrastination and laziness. In our school, plagiarism occurs more than anyone would like, but I will have to admit the majority of the students are much more clever about it than your everyday "print an essay offline and hand it in" scenario. Paraphrasing and the copy-and-paste function become the instant companion to any student wishing to get an assignment done, just to attain the goal of turning it in on time with minimum effort.

My general opinion is that plagiarism is something too idiotic to risk getting caught and being deemed an "immoral" student. I used to be one of the over-achievers who got by sometimes with easy As by cheating or copying work. I learned the hard way that this not only has large consequences on the teacher-student-parent trust level, but also for someone who spends so much time avoiding doing work, in the end nothing good comes to you in return. I am happy to say I do my own work now, and as an end result have improved my writing and work ethics immensely.

—*Beverly, age eighteen*

instance, might write an analysis of a different character from the General Prologue of *The Canterbury Tales* or a paraphrase of a different set of five lines from *A Midsummer Night's Dream*. At other times, I try to keep homework assignments personal ("What do you think is the most moving chapter in *The House on Mango Street* and why?") and in-class compositions more analytical ("Discuss the use of similes in *The House on Mango Street*."). The result? Fewer plagiarized homework assignments.

- Even on formal research assignments, I often ask students to provide an annotated bibliography. I like to make annotations personal as well as summative—I ask students not just to write a description of the source but also to state what they found valuable, interesting, or annoying about it.

### The Sampler Platter: Cutting and Pasting from Many Sources

According to Donald McCabe, "there's always been plagiarism" (NPR 2006). He quickly adds, however, that there has been a recent shift:

> I think what's different now is that the internet provides such a vast resource that's so easily accessible, that those students who are engaging in cut and paste plagiarism are doing it a lot more often, and I think that's where the explosion is.

Students who cut and paste from the Internet cleverly don't just take several items from the buffet table; they then cobble them together into something that sounds original and resists detection. To some, such work might even approach originality and represent a marketable skill. Take, for instance, reporter Jason Johnson (2007) of the *Washington Post*, who wrote an article titled "Cut-and-Paste Is a Skill, Too":

> My transfer from education to the world of business has reminded me just how important it is to be able to synthesize content from multiple sources, put structure around it and edit it into a coherent, single-voiced whole. Students who are able to create convincing amalgamations have gained a valuable business skill.

Johnson's got a point—there's some skill involved in pulling together separate parts to create an amalgam greater than its separate components. If you cite your sources, in fact, that process is called *research*. If, however, I'd simply included the previous two sentences Johnson wrote in this book without using quotation marks or setting them off as a block quotation, even if I'd listed his article in my bibliography, I'd be guilty of plagiarism—skill or no skill.

So what's involved? Most students who concoct what I call a sampler platter insert pieces—sentences or paragraphs—from various websites into a composite paper of their own design, not unlike the example *Huck Finn* paragraph with which I started this chapter. Some literally cut and paste the entire paper; others add sentences and transitions of their own design. It's a fairly common practice, too; in one study of high school juniors, 60 percent of the respondents admitted to, on some assignments, copying "a few sentences" without citation (McCabe 2005, 238).

The advent of the Internet makes cutting and pasting easier than ever; cutting and pasting itself is harder to detect than plagiarism of an entire paper, though electronic tools still help. But this sort of plagiarism isn't always as obvious to students themselves as one might think. Sure, highlighting two paragraphs of a Wikipedia entry and slapping it into the middle of an essay is wrong, and most students know it. But what about grabbing an image through a Google image search for a PowerPoint presentation? How about taking a statistic from a website that has attributed no source itself? Or what about material taken directly from the textbook as an answer to a factual question? Many students, especially those who operate in technology-rich learning environments, move information around so frequently for relatively minor assignments that they stop thinking of such infractions as plagiarism. Attribution, they might argue, is for research papers, not homework assignments.

Such thinking is probably at odds with the views of most teachers, and even more at odds with the views of most college professors, since at the collegiate level citation and attribution become matters not just of courtesy or honesty but of serious professional consequence. It's an issue worthy of more discussion (see the next chapter of this book for some thought about the ethics gap raised by teacher and student perspectives of plagiarism). Suffice it to say that the cut-and-paste approach is probably the most common method students use to compose papers quickly and efficiently and still maintain some control over the entire piece.

### Teaching Opportunities

To begin with, it's a good idea to reinforce the importance of bibliographies:

- Insist that students provide a bibliography not just for written assignments but also for classroom presentations, even those involving posters or digital slide shows.

---

**Voices from the Classroom**

I'm an early-career teacher, and I grew up with the Internet. When I was in high school it was easier to cheat because the Internet was new; no one expected it. I wasn't surprised to see plagiarism in our middle school, and I recognized that with middle schoolers if there's an easy way to do something, you're going to do it. You need an incentive for them *not* to plagiarize. But younger teachers, I think, often know better how to catch plagiarism using the Internet, because we've done it.

—*Middle school teacher*

Students in the habit of composing bibliographies are more likely to note their sources as they go along.

- Make the bibliography part of your scoring rubric. You might wish to weight it lower than the content of the paper itself, but the inclusion and correct formatting of a bibliography is worth including as part of a grade.

- Show students how easy it is to make a bibliography online using a site such as Easybib.com. There's little excuse for not including sources when the list is so simple to compile.

In addition to the bibliography, students need to understand the research process and why attribution is important. Chapter 5 includes more strategies for teaching the rules of citation and digital literacy skills. Also consider these precautions:

- Model the research process for students to be sure there is no misunderstanding about appropriate and inappropriate use of materials. If you have access to a computer with a projector, let students watch as you find a site (I often ask the students for a research topic so that they can see me research from a cold start), choose material to quote or paraphrase, keep track of relevant information in your own notes, and then compile a bibliography entry. You should also model this process using a print source.

- Make note taking a part of your assignments and assessments. Have students turn in notes not just with the final paper but as they research; peer editing is good practice with notes as well as rough drafts. Students can trade notes and track down one another's sources using them (this also helps with students who tend to make up false sources).

### Artificial Sweetener: The Power of Substitution

Here's a clever idea: Take a sentence from another source, like this suggestion for detecting plagiaries from a presentation called "Cheating 101: Detecting Plagiarized Papers":

When provided with a page from their paper that has words or passages removed, students can not fill in the blanks with the missing words or with reasonable synonyms. (Bates and Fain 2004)

Now rewrite it using a sort of fill-in-the-blank approach of your own:

When *given* a *passage* from their *essay* that has *terms* or *phrases taken out,* *pupils* can not fill in the blanks with the missing *terms* or with *logical* synonyms.

It's even easier if you have a built-in thesaurus with your word-processing program, like I do. A couple of keystrokes and the sentence doesn't come up instantly on Google or Turnitin.com. It's a lot of work, you might argue, but is it less work than writing an entire paper? You bet.

One glitch for students using this system is that the synonyms rarely sound quite right in the context of the new sentence (in the previous example, my computer suggested replacing *words* with *lexis*); another is that most students trying this approach get lazy enough that whole phrases still remain to be caught by an astute teacher or program. And, too, the citations don't change. There's no equivalent of a synonym in a bibliography. Finally, there's really no guarantee that the original source was a good answer to the essay question or prompt the student is trying to address.

Or, to stick with our metaphor: you can add an extra topping, you can switch the pepperoni for sausage, you can slice it in twelve pieces instead of eight, but no one doubts for a moment that you're still eating a pizza.

### Teaching Opportunities

At its worst, the practice of switching out words is primarily intended to deceive the reader. There's also the possibility, here, that students are attempting to paraphrase but doing so poorly (see the next section for more discussion of paraphrasing); more often, though, students sprinkle in synonyms in order to keep from being easily caught with a search engine. It's a tricky approach to plagiarism but one you can address.

- Be certain your students know that replacing individual words and phrases is still plagiarism. I usually save some blatant (and generally poorly written) samples with the authors' names removed to show future classes. I also like to show students examples from beyond our school—Kaavya Viswanathan or Doris Kearns Goodwin, for instance—and discuss the potential consequences of such practice.

- Try this: Write a paragraph on the board or photocopy it and hand it out to students. Have each student identify the most important sentence—the thesis or topic sentence. Then, on a note

## How Good Are Electronic Detection Services?

Remember the paragraph about *Huck Finn* at the start of this chapter? I tried checking it electronically myself in two ways:

1. *Google*. The good news: a quick Google search of the last sentence in the sample paragraph returned immediate results—the sentence was lifted directly out of the Spark-Notes chapter analysis for the novel (Martin and Martin n.d.). The bad news: having confirmed one example of plagiarism, I'm likely not to check the first, poorly written sentence. Read on.

2. *Turnitin.com*. Turnitin.com, in just a few seconds, accurately identified sentences 1, 2, 3, and 5 as plagiarized (yes, I composed sentence 4 myself). Take sentence one, for instance, the poorly written line about Pap's view of Huck's education, which I would probably have assumed the student wrote. While Turnitin.com did not find the original source of the sentence (a pretty lousy paper from a term paper mill called 123helpme.com [n.d.]), it did make a 100 percent match to identical sentences in essays submitted by three other high school teachers around the country as well as to an earlier submission of the same paragraph I made myself. It also correctly identified, interestingly, the online text from which I lifted the precisely quoted material from the novel itself. Overall, a very useful report—and it took me, all told, about three minutes to submit the paper and review the results.

One must still be careful to study the report carefully—the site flags quoted as well as unquoted material. And, if a student has posted his own work on the Internet, Turnitin.com might even catch that source and flag a paper for plagiarism because of it. Finally a drawback of all electronic detection services and software is that work must be typed before it can be submitted. If you're dealing with large chunks of potentially plagiarized material but the student paper is handwritten, you're stuck either retyping the text or resorting to searching for a small piece at a time.

*Note*: The actual sources I used to create that paragraph are listed in the "Works Cited" section at the end of this chapter. They include a free student essay (sentence 1), the SparkNotes analysis (sentences 2 and 5), and an online version of the text from the University of Virginia Library (sentence 3; Cope 1995).

card, sticky note, or scrap of paper, have each student write down any three—and only three—nonconsecutive words from the paragraph that sum up the idea. Then have students rewrite the topic sentence using those three words but no others from the original. Share the sentences with partners, read them out loud, or write them on the board and discuss. Be sure to point out that the new sentences still use three words from the original source that may require citation or substitution.

- The paraphrasing practice suggested at the end of the next section can be helpful here, as well.

### The Problem with Paraphrasing

The problem with paraphrasing, frankly, is that most students haven't learned to do it well. Paraphrasing is a legitimate practice so long as credit is given. The Harvard University guide for students called *Writing with Internet Sources*, for instance, warns students of the dangers of excessive paraphrasing, paraphrasing without citation, rewording material too closely, and failing to keep notes of material that might come up in a written assignment (Burg et al 2007). And, just to make the point, I paraphrased the guide in my previous sentence instead of quoting it.

Figure 2.1 offers three versions of the same material, taken from a chapter on writing research papers in *The Bedford Introduction to Literature* (Meyer 1993). Take a look, especially, at the *incorrect* paraphrase and you'll see how easy it is for students to slightly reword a passage without attribution or quotation. (All classroom examples and assignments are cited according to Modern Library Association rules.)

Paraphrasing is, in fact, great reading practice. It's also a necessary and valuable skill for research writing; it helps students maintain a balance between quoting long passages of dreary material and failing to attribute their ideas. Paraphrasing is not quite the same as summarizing, which usually focuses on a single main idea rather than a restatement of the majority of information in a passage; each is a valuable tool for the writer.

### Teaching Opportunities

Figure 2.2 helps students focus on three aspects of incorporating another text into one's own work:

- First, the handout encourages students to consider the difference between paraphrasing and plagiarizing by having them not just reword but restate the passage.

- Next, the handout guides students in quoting and attributing ideas from the original passage.

| Original Source | Incorrect Paraphrase | Correct Paraphrase |
|---|---|---|
| "Some mention should be made of the notion of common knowledge before we turn to the standard format for documenting sources. Observations and facts that are widely known and routinely included in many of your sources do not require documentation. It is not necessary to cite a source for the fact that Alfred, Lord Tennyson was born in 1809 or that Ernest Hemingway loved to fish and hunt." (Meyer 2076) | It's worth noting that in a research paper, common knowledge need not be documented. Data that is universally learned, like the date of Tennyson's birth or Hemingway's love of hunting, is exempt from the need for documentation. | According to Meyer, facts and observations that are widely known, such as Tennyson's birth or Hemingway's love of hunting, constitute a body of common knowledge that does not require documentation (2076). |

*Figure 2.1*

- Finally, the handout guides students toward the most important aspect of paraphrasing—the skill of using a paraphrase in conjunction with one's own ideas about a topic to produce a new, original piece of writing.

You can, of course, complete this sort of practice in your own classroom at any time with a variety of passages that might appeal to your particular students.

### What's So Good About Home Cooking, Anyway? The Other End of the Paraphrasing Problem

So, you're having dinner at a friend's house and you praise the soup.

"Campbell's," your friend says.

Later, you offer kudos on the main course.

"KFC," your friend responds.

The dessert?

"Betty Crocker."

# Paraphrasing Practice

## Important Terms

*Plagiarizing:* copying words or ideas that aren't your own without citing the source

*Allusion:* a reference to another story or character

*Paraphrasing:* restating an idea in your own words

*Citing:* noting in the text (usually by putting the author's name in parentheses) the source of an idea or quotation

*First, read the passage below:*

Plagiarism seeks to conceal the source, while allusion seeks to reveal it. In creative writing (poetry, fiction, drama, memoir), you may indeed include allusions. These are references to other texts that extend your meaning. But in academic writing (essays, research, argumentation, lab reports), you must document all of your sources. ("Academic Integrity")

*Now, answer these questions:*

1. According to the paragraph, what is the difference between plagiarism and allusion?

_____

_____

_____

2. Find the most important sentence and write it below.

_____

_____

_____

_____

3. Circle the most important three or four words in that sentence and write them below.

_____

4. Paraphrase the sentence you identified in question 2. You may use two words from your answer to question 3 *but no other words from the original sentence.*

_____

_____

_____

_____

*Figure 2.2*

# Paraphrasing Practice, continued

## Citation Reminders

- For MLA format, put the author's name and page number in parentheses: (Smith 92).

- Place the period after the parentheses (see above). There is no comma between the name and page number.

- If you use the author's name in the sentence, you don't have to include it at the end.

- If you access the source online, no page number is needed.

- Remember to place the source in your bibliography, as well.

5. Write a sentence of your own in which you quote from the paragraph. Use quotation marks and a citation at the end of the sentence.

_____

_____

_____

6. In the space below, describe one instance in which the author of the paragraph might be _wrong_. When might you use an allusion in academic writing?

_____

_____

_____

_____

7. Now a write a paragraph of your own. In your writing, comment on the original paragraph—do you mostly agree or mostly disagree? At some point in your answer, either quote the original paragraph and cite it or paraphrase the original paragraph and cite it.

_____

_____

_____

_____

_____

_____

_____

## Works Cited

Grace Hauenstein Library. n.d. "Academic Integrity." Aquinas College. www.aquinas.edu/library/plagiarism.html (accessed Feb. 18, 2008).

_Figure 2.2_

Feel satisfied? Maybe in terms of hunger, but what about in spirit? Honesty without originality simply falls flat. The same is true in writing: the answer to plagiarism is not simply to quote *everything*, though some students seem to think that works. I've read student papers where an entire paragraph consisted of nothing but quoted material:

> One author notes that "some mention should be made of the notion of common knowledge before we turn to the standard format for documenting sources. Observations and facts that are widely known and routinely included in many of your sources do not require documentation." (Meyer 2076)

Though technically correct, such a paragraph does little to advance an original argument. For the same reason that paraphrasing needs to include a focus not just on restatement but on incorporation and relationship to the student's thesis, quotation must be tuned to the thesis as well—the point needs to be clear to students that a piece of academic writing is part of a discussion in which other voices are acknowledged but not simply regurgitated.

### Teaching Opportunities

As with paraphrasing, I find it beneficial to have students identify the key phrase of a passage and use it in a quoted line. Because many students like to quote statements that are much lengthier than necessary, I place a six- to eight-word limit on such phrases, then insist that the student's *own* sentence be at least twice that number of words. The idea is to get students not just to quote but to include some analysis or response in the sentence containing the quote. For example:

> Meyer notes that "facts that are widely known" constitute a body of common knowledge and therefore need not be documented, but how does an author determine what is "widely known" if he or she didn't know the fact before reading another source? (2076)

With advanced students, I push this assignment further: identify three words from the passage, I instruct them, and then quote them in a nonconsecutive manner in your own writing:

> Meyer includes not only "facts" but also "observations" (2076) in his definition of common knowledge, but the assumption that numerous writers will observe the same details "routinely" seems to be a large leap.

The goal, ultimately, is to encourage students to think as they research, write, and incorporate material and not simply to strive to include source material of whatever sort in the papers they produce.

## Too Many Chefs: More Types of Dishonesty in Writing

If plagiarizing means taking credit for work that isn't yours, can we use the term for the appropriation of work that never existed in the first place? Maybe or maybe not, but the fact remains that there are other examples of academic dishonesty that, whether or not they constitute technical plagiarism, certainly come close and occur for similar reasons. Some students, for instance:

> ### Voices from the Classroom
>
> When I write papers in which outside sources are used, I usually just copy and paste the URL and go back to the site later when I am ready to write the bibliography. Some sites, however, allow people to see it for a limited time, but after that they have to have a password and agree to all this stuff to see it again. This occurred with me a couple of months ago. I was typing up the bibliography and I clicked on the URL I had pasted in my paper. The window came up saying that this site was blocked. The quote I had received from the site, however, was really good and fit perfectly for my paper. So, I changed the internal citations, and said they were from a different document.
>
> —*Janice, age seventeen*

- make up sources completely;
- include in-text citations for sources that don't appear in a bibliography (and vice versa);
- quote from one source only, but change the in-text citations to reflect numerous real sources that appear in the bibliography;
- write papers with no copied material but with an idea that is organized and proven in a way that mimics another source (i.e., plagiarize an outline);
- have parents or relatives write or heavily revise papers for them; or
- self-plagiarize by submitting their own papers for multiple courses or assignments.

Each of these cases involves a slightly different purpose and technique, but the end result of all is deception and a failure to follow the proper procedures of attribution. The best answer to such examples of dishonesty is probably to teach the research and citation process carefully and deliberately; it's also important, however, to find out *why* students are engaging in these practices, whether they're intentional or unintentional efforts to deceive, and whether simple correction and education might fix the problem in the future; those issues are the focus of the next chapter of this book.

## Final Thoughts About Responses to Plagiarism

At the beginning of this chapter, I recounted one of the too-frequent moments in which I realize a student has plagiarized all or part of an essay. It's important, at such a moment, to find proof, to discover how the student plagiarized and whether or not an accusation is sustainable. It's just as important, though, to reflect on my own position as teacher at such a moment. What's the role I want to play? Am I willing, at five o'clock, to take off my teacher cap and put on the one of academic policeman? For the sake of my students, can I afford not to?

I believe that the most dangerous moment for any teacher in dealing with a potential case of plagiarism is the moment immediately following the discovery. Later, with time to reflect on how and why a student committed an offense, teachers often make decisions in the best interest of education and consistent classroom policy. In the heat of the moment, though, when one finds an example of dishonesty in a paper, it's easy to get zealous, and perhaps overzealous, about proving the crime and prosecuting the offender. So, at five o'clock, with a copied essay on *Huck Finn* in my hands, what do I do?

First I look for the proof, because I just have to know. But then? Take a breath, close up shop, and put it aside for another day. It's tough not to take the paper home with me—not just physically, but emotionally. And sometimes, honestly, I fail. But I know that I'm a better teacher when I don't immediately pull out the red pen, grab the grade book, or write an email to my principal. I know I serve my students better when I give myself time to plan how to approach them and what my position will be. "How?" is a good question, but it's not the only one we need to ask.

## Works Cited

123helpme.com. n.d. "Free Essays—Survival in *The Adventures of Huckleberry Finn.*" www.123helpme.com/view.asp?id=16713 (accessed Feb 18, 2008).

Bates, Peggy, and Margaret Fain. 2004. "Cheating 101: Detecting Plagiarized Papers." Kimbel Library, Coastal Carolina University. Nov. 4. www.coastal.edu/library/presentations/plagiarz.html (accessed Feb. 18, 2008).

———. 2006. "Cheating 101: Internet Paper Mills." Kimbel Library, Coastal Carolina University. Oct. 18. www.coastal.edu/library/presentations/mills2.html (accessed Feb. 18, 2008).

Burg, Barbara, et al. 2007. *Writing with Internet Sources: A Guide for Harvard Students.* Cambridge: Expository Writing Program, Harvard College.

Campbell, Don. 2007. "The Plagiarism Plague." *National Crosstalk.* www.highereducation.org/crosstalk/ct0106/news0106-plagiarism.shtml (accessed Feb. 18, 2008).

College Administration Publications. n.d. "New Research on Academic Integrity: The Success of 'Modified' Honor Codes." www.collegepubs.com/ref/ SFX000515.shtml (accessed Mar. 23, 2008).

Cope, Virginia H. 1995. "Mark Twain's Huckleberry Finn: Text, Illustrations, and Early Reviews." University of Virginia. http://etext.virginia.edu/twain/ huckfinn.html (accessed Feb. 18, 2008).

Grace Hauenstein Library. n.d. "Academic Integrity." Aquinas College. www.aquinas.edu/library/plagiarism.html (accessed Feb. 18, 2008).

iParadigms. 2007. "Did You Know?" *Plagiarism.org.* www.plagiarism.org/ learning_center/did_you_know.html (accessed Feb. 18, 2008).

———. 2008. Turnitin.com. www.turnitin.com/ (accessed Feb. 10, 2008).

ItchyBrainsCentral. n.d. "Academic Writing by ItchyBrainsCentral." www .itchybrainscentral.com/ (accessed Feb. 18, 2008).

Johnson, Jason. 2007. "Cut-and-Paste Is a Skill, Too." *Washington Post* Mar. 27. www.washingtonpost.com/wpdyn/content/article/2007/03/23/ AR2007032301612_pf.html (accessed Feb. 18, 2008).

Martin, Melissa and Stephanie Martin. n.d. "SparkNote on *The Adventures of Huckleberry Finn.*" www.sparknotes.com/lit.huckfin (accessed Feb. 18, 2008).

McCabe, Donald. 2005. "Cheating: Why Students Do It and How We Can Help Them Stop." In *Guiding Students From Cheating and Plagiarism to Honesty and Integrity: Strategies for Change,* comp. Ann Lathrop and Kathleen Foss. Westport, CT: Libraries Unlimited.

McCabe, Donald L., and Linda K. Trevino. 1993. "Academic Dishonesty: Honor Codes and Other Contextual Influences." *Journal of Higher Education* 5: 522–538.

Meyer, Michael. 1993. *The Bedford Introduction to Literature.* 3d ed. Boston: Bedford Books.

Muha, Dave. 2003. "New Study Confirms Internet Plagiarism is Prevalent." Office of Media Relations. Rutgers University. Aug. 28. http://ur.rutgers.edu/ medrel/viewArticle.html?ArticleID=3408 (accessed Feb. 19, 2008).

National Public Radio (NPR). 2006. "Cut and Paste Plagiarism." *Talk of the Nation.* Feb. 14.

Tenbusch, James P. "Stem the tide of technology-assisted plagiarism and tackle incidents properly when they occur." *Scholastic* (2002). http://www2.scholastic .com/browse/article.jsp?id=462. (accessed Mar. 29, 2008).

U.S. National Library of Medicine. 2008. "Sickle-Cell Anemia." Medline Plus. Mar. 14. www.nlm.nih.gov/medlineplus/sicklecellanemia.html (accessed Mar. 19, 2008).

Wikipedia contributors. 2008. "Sickle-Cell Disease." Wikipedia. Mar. 18. http:// en.wikipedia.org/wiki/Sickle-cell_disease (accessed Mar. 19, 2008).

# 3 *Shades of Gray*

## *Why Students Plagiarize*

Let's begin this chapter with a hypothesis: no student would choose to cheat if it seemed easier not to.

I know. You're already mustering counterarguments in your head; it's what teachers do. And I'll admit that there exists, in all probability, a fractional minority of students who cheat just to see if they can get away with it or possibly even out of spite. But the vast majority of students, I believe, cheat for reasons that, in one way or another, make sense to them as they commit the offense.

Plagiarism's a more difficult issue, though, than some forms of cheating. For one thing, the rules of attribution include some aspects that can seem subtle or even downright arcane to students. For another, assignments and expectations in middle and high school are rarely as clear-cut as they may be at the college level. Most of the research on plagiarism has involved studies at colleges, where writing assignments tend to come in lump packages—essays, research papers, lab reports—rather than in untidy smaller units such as daily vocabulary homework or current events reports. What research there is on plagiarism in high school is often mixed in with a larger study about cheating in general, but cheating in high school (and middle school) includes much more than plagiarism; statistics about the two issues shouldn't be confused.

It's tough, then, to tell how much plagiarism occurs in middle and high school, and it's tougher to sort out exactly how and how often it occurs. It's worth investigating, however, *why* it occurs. If we can accept that students cheat for a reason, and if we can accept that, in general, they'd rather do their work honestly and by the rules if it were not more difficult to do so, then perhaps we can seek to remove the reasons for plagiarism and replace them with reasons to write original work.

## TOP TEN: Reasons Students Give for Plagiarizing

1. Confusion about the procedure:

   "I don't know what all those terms mean—*citation, attribution, quotation*—what's the difference?"

   "I thought I didn't need to cite facts."

   "I didn't think I needed to cite for minor assignments."

   "I couldn't find the source again after I put it in my notes—I didn't think it mattered."

2. Procrastination:

   "The deadline crept up on me."

3. Pressure:

   "My parents want me to make good grades."

   "If I don't make a good grade, I'll lose my privileges."

4. Avoidance:

   "I thought I could get away with it."

   "I didn't want to do the assignment."

5. Confusion about the assignment:

   "I didn't understand the directions."

   "I didn't want to use too many sources."

   "I thought we were *supposed* to copy the answers from the book."

6. Student culture:

   "In my culture, it's considered flattering to use someone else's words."

   "We just don't cite that way in schools in my country."

   "My English language skills aren't good enough to understand the sources."

7. School culture:

   "Everyone else does it—why should I suffer for being honest?"

   "Teachers don't really care—in fact, they encourage it."

   "It's no big deal—that's the way the system works."

8. Self-doubt:

   "I'm no good at writing."

   "I'll never get it right, anyway."

9. Disdain for the assignment:

   "When will I ever need to know this stuff?"

   "The content doesn't matter—I'm just here for the grade."

   "This is just busywork."

10. Collaboration:

    "I thought we could work together."

## The Murky Waters of Middle and High School

"It's like our history class yesterday," Amanda says to me when I ask her class about cheating in our school. "We were in the library working on a quiz and the teacher walked out for a minute. We all immediately started talking about the answers even though she told us to be quiet before she left."

"You all cheated?" I ask.

"Well, sort of. But it was an open-book quiz, so we were all going to get the same answers anyway. She even took the questions straight out of the book."

Another student, Brittany, chimes in, "The questions were word for word from the book. We were just supposed to write down the next few sentences. It was dumb."

"Does that mean you plagiarized?" I ask.

"Maybe," Brittany answers. "I hadn't thought about it that way. But, uh, if we plagiarized, then so did the teacher, because she copied the exact words from the book, too. And anyway, we all knew the source. What, were we supposed to do an MLA citation after every answer?"

Amanda adds, "That's the thing about our classes. We all know where the stuff's coming from. It's like when we copy stuff into a PowerPoint, like you were talking

---

### Voices from the Classroom

Plagiarism at our school is often taken too seriously. I have a different definition of plagiarism than [my school]. Copying hw [homework] from another student, i.e. vocabulary, is not what I call plagiarism. Every person should get the same answers anyway if it is correct. I also consider vocabulary and chapter questions busywork, and it should be counted for participation not accuracy. Copying something out of a book but changing the words around is not what I consider plagiarism because they are my own words, but the idea is coming from someone else.

—*Shawna, age seventeen*

about. I could always give you all the web pages, but who really cares? We're just going to trash it the next day."

"OK," I say. "But do you think that when you and a teacher copy straight from the book, that might make some students think it's OK to copy out of the book for other assignments?"

"Absolutely," Amanda says. "I think that happens all the time."

Brittany shrugs. "It's still no big deal."

I'm not entirely in agreement with these two high school students, but I see their point. There are a lot of gray areas in middle and high school. Consider the following scenarios, all taken from examples given to me by actual students:

> ### Voices from the Classroom
>
> I have a lot of parents who do the work for the kids. You can't Google it, so I keep copies of in-class writing to compare to writing from home. Nine times out of ten, the kid will say, "Yeah, Grandma wrote that for me." And then they say, "She said it was OK, so how could that be bad?" You have to call the parent and approach [it] from the angle of what the child is learning rather than the grades. That's really hard.
>
> *—Sixth-grade teacher*

- An English teacher allows students to work in pairs to define vocabulary words, but is upset when the pairs divide the list in half, with each student looking up half the words and copying the rest of the list from the other student.

- A middle school language arts teacher does not allow her students to use online study guides but gets her quiz questions directly from an online source (and the students know it).

- A science teacher gives a sample lab to students and has them copy portions of the text directly into their own lab reports, while other sections must be original.

- A single student, in the course of one day, is asked to use three different formats for attribution—and can fail an assignment in a social studies class if the attribution is wrong, but will only have points deducted for providing no citations at all.

- An art teacher copies and pastes images from the Internet onto a test for students without attribution but expects students to attribute images in their homework.

Students see, at best, a level of confusion in such scenarios and, at worst, hypocrisy. As a classroom teacher, I can envision justifications for most of these situations, in the same way I understand that photocopying a page of a text for use in classroom discussion is different—legally and ethically—from copying a page of text into an essay without acknowledgment of the source. Such distinctions aren't always as clear to students. Most adolescents understand the concept of copying and get that wholesale plagiarism is generally against the rules, but many students nevertheless have trouble navigating the system of acceptability and responsibility in attribution, largely because of the inconsistent models with which they are presented.

## Good Intentions

Most writers about plagiarism agree that a discussion of intent is important. A professor from my own alma mater, for instance, suggests that "disregarding intent steers the case to conviction almost by default" but that some colleges may not focus on intent because "the one thing a college must protect is its reputation" (Harris 2007). In other words, at the collegiate level, the importance of how the integrity of the institution is perceived may outweigh the importance of careful consideration of facts. Middle and high school teachers may be less concerned with an institution's reputation and more concerned with the reputation of their own teaching or with the student's education; still, it's unclear how much weight to give to the idea of intentions. One thing's certain: at all levels, there's uncertainty among individual teachers faced with deciding cases of plagiarism that might harm a student's grade, reputation, and future.

What's more, many online sites about plagiarism (just about every college or public library has one) neatly divide all plagiarism into intentional and unintentional acts. In almost every case, the exceptions being egregious examples in the vein of downloading full term papers, I'd like to see the word *probably* added to those labels, but it rarely is. Knowing the intent of a student and inferring intent from the *type* of plagiarism are quite different. Consider what impact such confusion between motivation and product might bring about in your classroom—as one writer notes, it creates a situation where intentions may be wildly misdiagnosed,

> with the terms "intentional" and "unintentional" functioning as convenient labels for texts rather than as descriptions of writers. . . . As a result, the recommended teachers' responses to patchwriting (which is classified as "unintentional" plagiarism) often have little bearing on the actual needs of the student writers. (Howard 1999, 109)

In other words, if we don't know *why*—and if we don't know whether the student *intended* to cheat—we can only punish; we can't educate.

I prefer to think of intent as a spectrum rather than a duality. Take a look at Figure 3.1 and consider the range of possibilities. Some acts of plagiarism are clearly intentional; others seem almost certainly acciden-

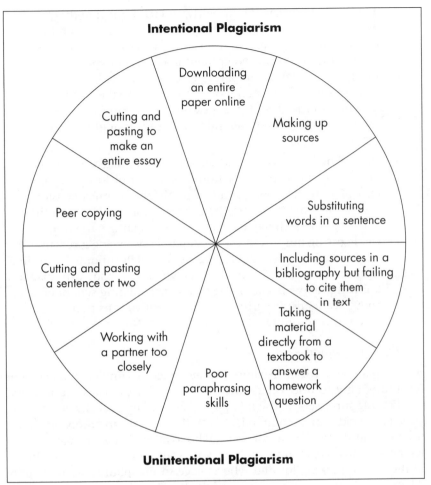

*Figure 3.1 Intentional and Unintentional Plagiarism*

tal. Most, however, fall into a gray area in between—an area in which such aspects as understanding of the assignment or previous experience with teacher expectations become extremely important in determining intentions.

It's important here to note the following:

- It's possible to be mistaken about intentions based solely on the nature of the writing. I imagine, based on my experience and discussions with students, that most of the time students don't think of copying from a textbook to answer a simple question as a form of plagiarism—frequently, in fact, I imagine they're expected to do just that. But there may be times when the expectations change, when the student is expected to paraphrase and when the assignment makes that expectation clear. In such cases, failure to paraphrase becomes either a matter of student misunderstanding or of an intentional effort to sidestep the rules of the class. If we lock ourselves into thinking about intent as static, we are bound to misread student motivation in many cases.

- Discussing intent is not the same thing as discussing consequence. Just because an action falls higher or lower on the circle in Figure 3.1 does not mean punishments must be more severe for some instances than others, nor does it mean that teaching is less effective for the actions near the top of the circle. Figuring out intent is one step in considering a reaction to plagiarism, but it should not be the sole determining factor in a teacher's response. Even students who download entire papers, knowing full well that doing so means violating school policies about academic integrity, may have motivations that should be taken into account.

### Teaching Opportunities

A few years ago I took a short survey called a conflict management inventory, only to discover that my personality type leads me to avoid conflict. Big surprise—my own family jokes that my checklist for conflict goes (1) avoid; (2) accommodate; (3) flee. There are probably other teachers out there like me, the ones who assume that every parent conference will involve an irate mother who wants you tarred and feathered in the school parking lot and who engage in disciplining students only when they have to, as part of the job (I'm usually wrong on the first count, and I recognize the necessity of enforcing school rules, of course, but I don't *enjoy* that part of the job). Other teachers never hesitate and don't even seem bothered by the kinds of conflicts that can easily arise in any school.

The thing about plagiarism is that it's one time that hesitation pays off. That's not just because any teacher making an accusation of plagiarism needs certain proof (or the knowledge that proof can't be found) before confronting a student. It's also because the confrontation itself can often produce no result other than defensiveness, even if the student admits right away to the dishonesty. Actually, getting students to admit guilt is rarely the difficulty in cases of plagiarism. The problem comes from the shame, guilt, and inevitable consequences that follow an accusation. That's not to say, again, that the consequences shouldn't apply, but consider this model of a teacher-student discussion about plagiarism:

accusation

↓

admission or denial

↓

consequence

And this one:

raising a question or problem

↓

explanation of student thinking

↓

explanation of teacher thinking

learning     consequence

This model of response to student wrongdoing probably applies across the board, but I believe it's more important with cases of plagiarism than say, gum chewing or scribbling on the walls of the school bathroom. Plagiarism includes so many shades of gray that determining intention is a key element of helping students learn and correct; punishment alone won't do it.

The form in Figure 3.2 is designed to help teachers gather information before committing to a course of action that might well involve parents and administrators. It's not meant to replace a system of consequence but to augment one, to ensure that the proceedings are in the best interest of the student as well as school policy.

When I suspect a case of plagiarism, I don't grade the paper. Instead, I simply attach this form to a copy of the student's work (I keep the original) and hand it back *right away*. While the student is completing the form, I gather evidence of my own using a search engine, Turnitin.com, or whatever other sources I deem necessary. The purpose is twofold; on the one hand, it helps me understand the student's position and determine intent, while on the other, the process of filling out the form gives the student time to reflect on the offense. Rather than blurting out a lie that will compound the original error (often the first defense of a guilty student), she considers and reconsiders and, more often than not, writes

## Assignment Explanation Form

Student Name: _____

Teacher and Course Name: _____

Date: _____

Assignment: _____

I noticed the following as I graded this assignment:

_____ Some passages appear to come directly from another document.

_____ Some passages seem to be very close in structure or idea to those in another document.

_____ Some citations appear to be missing or incorrect.

_____ Some bibliography entries appear to be missing or incorrect.

The spaces below offer you an opportunity to correct any misunderstandings before I move forward with my response to this assignment. This form does not reflect any intended grade or course of action on my part; it is simply an effort to collect information.

1. Please explain the process you used in your research and writing for this assignment.

_____

_____

_____

2. Was there anything you misunderstood about the assignment or its parameters?

_____

_____

_____

3. Please describe any external pressures or factors you would like me to consider as I choose how to respond to your work (for instance: deadline pressures, concerns about your grades, or descriptions of collaborative processes you used).

_____

_____

_____

4. Please sign your name below.

_____

*Figure 3.2*

## YOU NEED TO KNOW: Memory Lapse, or Lapse in Judgment?

Plagiarists throughout history have claimed innocence by maintaining that they didn't recall actually getting material from another source. Is there truly such a thing as unconscious plagiarism? According to recent studies reported in the *Boston Globe*, the phenomenon—called *cryptomnesia* by experts—may be more common than we think, occurring in 8 to 12 percent of subjects in one test and up to 20 percent in others (Goldberg 2006).

One interesting line of thought arising from such tests is summed up by researcher Richard Marsh in the same article: "when people are busy trying to be creative, they tend to fail to consider where their ideas come from and can inadvertently steal." Learning to combat such tendencies is partly a matter of training—copying down a URL or book title in one's notes beside a summary of material without slowing down the creative process, then formatting a full bibliographical entry later on, for instance. The idea of such inadvertent theft ought also, however, to warn us against assuming that every plagiarized word is a malicious crime.

down a truthful answer on the form. If the student's answer includes claims of innocence, I can always produce my evidence later on (or, if I have no evidence, consider taking the student at her word).

Of course, another strong means of battling unintentional plagiarism is making sure that students understand the rules of citation, quotation, paraphrasing, and attribution. I often show students a version of the pie chart in Figure 3.1 close to the start of a course and answer any questions they have about the definition of plagiarism and how I'll respond to it. I also make sure they have some resources for citing correctly.

## Listening to Reason

One of the most famous recent cases of battling Internet plagiarism at the high school level involves a teacher named Christine Pelton, who turned to Turnitin.com when she suspected widespread plagiarism in response to a major assignment in her biology class. Almost one-quarter of her sophomores, it turned out, had plagiarized material from the Internet. What was really interesting about this case was that Pelton had had students *and* parents sign a contract that included a plagiarism rule at the start of the year. Yet after she failed the students, parents appealed to the school board, who overruled Pelton, changed the grades, and allowed students who would have failed the course to pass. Pelton resigned immediately; other teachers resigned at the end of the school year.

The parents' contention, in part, was that their children hadn't been taught how *not* to plagiarize. One student spoke anonymously to the CBS show *48 Hours* about the situation:

> "I was kind of upset 'cause I was pretty sure I did't do it," he says, claiming he copied from the Internet but didn't plagiarize. . . . "I put that as two different sentences," he says. "So it's not like I copied it straight from the Web site. I changed it into two different sentences." (2002)

There's much about this case to consider: the roles of students, parents, administration, and the teacher are all worthy of contemplation. There's an interesting conundrum involved in how the problem was addressed; because the value of the assignment in question was lowered by the school board, students who made high scores in the first place, students who *didn't* plagiarize, saw their scores go down. And, too, there's a question of how such a case, with the national media attention it brought, can destroy a school community and a school's reputation.

But for all the difficulties raised by the case, and as fully as most outside observers felt that the school board acted inappropriately (the deans of the University of Kansas even sent a chastising letter to the board), it's clear to me that the student quoted previously really didn't *get* the concept of plagiarism. Was it discussed in his class at some point? I don't

## My School, My Classroom

My survey of around two hundred students, grades 7–12, in my own school produced data for the following two charts. The first chart shows the responses of these students to the question, "Why do you think most students at our school plagiarize?" Notice how little credence these students give to the notion that confusion or school culture encourage academic dishonesty (though it is important to note that student perception of motivations is not necessarily accurate). The second chart shows the responses of the students to the question, "How serious an offense do you think it is to copy a homework assignment or essay from a peer?" Interestingly, while only a few students classified this act as "not serious at all," only a few considered it to be "very serious," with the vast majority falling somewhere in the middle.

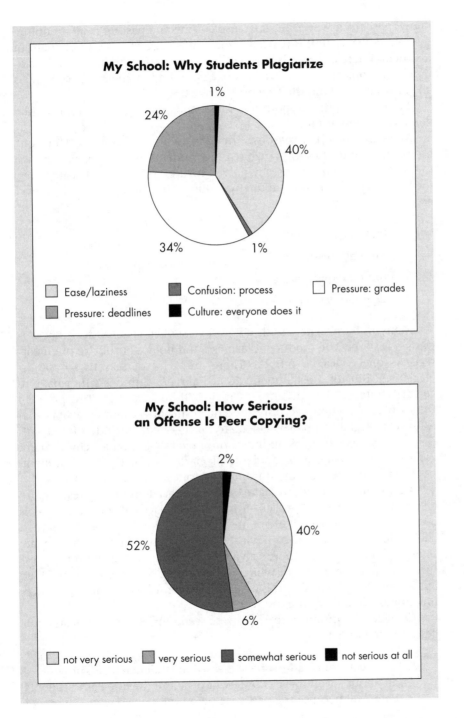

know; perhaps it was. Does it excuse cutting and pasting from an online source? Probably not. But what it may do is suggest to us an element of instruction that's often missing—a clear explanation of process, expectations, and consequences. The idea of a contract is a good one, so long as all parties understand the fine print.

So here's another hypothesis: some students plagiarize because they don't know how *not* to.

What are the other reasons? Though I've already used the "Top Ten" list in this chapter to summarize reasons students give for plagiarism, we can boil those explanations down even further to four simple categories, the first of which stems from the hypothesis I just brought up. Plagiarism occurs because of

1. student confusion;

2. external pressures;

3. cultural expectations; or

4. perceptions of ease.

Many of the teachers with whom I've spoken seem to feel that plagiarism is simply the product of laziness, and no doubt they're often correct. As one colleague put it, "There are a lot of reasons to *consider* plagiarism. But for most students to actually do it, things either have to get desperate or the student has to just think it's OK." The problem comes when teachers see only the end result of a chain of events that leads to a plagiarized paper. For many of us—and I include myself—it's easy to view plagiarism as an indicator of overall academic achievement: good students write, poor students plagiarize. Even the good student, however, often feels assaulted from many sides (see Figure 3.3).

Again, the goal is not to make excuses for academic dishonesty but to determine how we can prevent it in the first place—if the student feels bombarded by disparate elements and expectations, teachers face a choice: force the student to navigate those pressures or try to alleviate some of them. Certainly there's a value to learning to cope with the pressures of schooling, many of which only increase as students grow older, but it's also worth considering whether we contribute to such pressures unwittingly and, therefore, unnecessarily.

Consider, for instance, the following scenarios, which actual students described to me:

1. You've assigned a four-page essay that students have known about for several weeks. A few days before the due date, students complain because the paper is due on the same day as the school

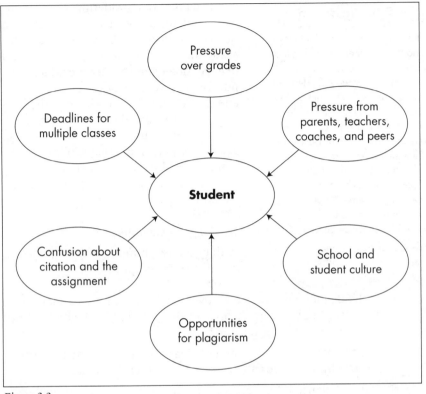

*Figure 3.3*

science fair, which they've also known about for weeks. Do you change the deadline?

2. An ESL student who works with a tutor regularly turns in work that is written in far better language than he uses when he writes on his own. The week the major research paper is due, the tutor will be out of town and unable to help the student. Do you require the student to write the paper on his own? Offer to help him yourself? Extend the deadline?

3. The girls soccer team is traveling to the state tournament over the weekend. The players promise to have their written work, which is due on Monday, turned in on time and they claim they don't want extra time; you know, however, that they will have little free time and will be together for most of the trip, and you already suspect one of the players of copying another's paper. How do you proceed?

### Voices from the Classroom

If you have a learning disability and it takes you twice as long to remember something that you have to know by tomorrow, of course you're tempted by the easier way. Students of all kinds, including those with disabilities, talk about information *they* don't find valuable to them and how for some reason that makes it acceptable to cheat. If they see it as busywork, they may not think twice. And education— what we do with information—is changing around them. They think, "Why memorize when I can access this anytime?" There *is* still value in memorization—for the brain, for later tasks—but that's not the perception.

*—Middle school special needs teacher*

The point of considering such scenarios is not to arrive at a correct answer, nor is it to displace the responsibility for academic integrity from the student. I believe, however, that teachers face such puzzles on a regular basis (I certainly do) and that we need to be aware of the possible results of our decisions. We want to be, and need to be, fair. We want to instill a sense of personal responsibility in students. We also want them to do their own work. The conundrum is achieving all of those goals at once.

### Teaching Opportunities

With every assignment I make, I try to ask myself a series of questions:

- Is the deadline reasonable? Have I checked with the students to make sure the deadline works for them? Will I be flexible or firm if I'm asked for an extension?

- Are the steps of the assignment clear? Have I left time for students with questions about the steps to seek out help?

- Have I balanced the weight of the grade the assignment will receive with the care I will take in providing steps that discourage plagiarism—having students show me physical copies of sources, compose outlines and drafts, or craft thesis statements in class, for instance?

- Have I made my expectations about group work and acceptable use of external resources clear on this particular assignment?

- Have I invited any students who might have concerns or external pressures to talk to me *before* the assignment is due, even if I'm unwilling to extend the deadline?

- Have I explained the motivation behind making this assignment to be sure students don't consider it busywork? Do I have student buy-in on the importance of this assignment, and if not, what can I do to achieve that buy-in?

In a later chapter, I further discuss making assignments; these questions aren't generally meant to alter my assignments so much as to make sure I've communicated clearly with students and done my best to cir-

cumvent those pressures that I can. Sometimes deadlines matter to me greatly
because, for instance, I need time to get a
batch of essays finished before parent conferences or the end of the grading period.
At other times, I don't really care whether
the papers are due on Wednesday or
Thursday because there's no chance I'll
even look at them until the weekend—
but the students may very well care, and
not just because they're procrastinating.

In fact, as often as possible, I involve
classes in setting up deadlines for the
entire course. I'll list the work that is due
on the board, give students a calendar for the grading period, and ask
them to suggest due dates for various assignments. Most classes aren't
dumb, and they won't put off everything until the last minute (I
wouldn't let them, anyway—one stipulation is always that I must have a
reasonable amount of time to comment on and grade all papers). The
result is a sense of ownership and understanding on the part of the students, as well as an inability to complain about due dates as they come
up. Does this practice discourage plagiarism? Not entirely, but it doesn't
hurt—students who take part in planning are more likely to remember
due dates and adhere to them. They also tend to understand the purpose
and placement of assignments as they arise.

> ### Voices from the Classroom
>
> I think the pressure to do well on what we are assigned leads to plagiarism. Pressure from parents, teachers, administration, colleges, and even pressure from our peers. People think I'm smart and I feel that I have to live up to that at times. I don't plagiarize unless there is no other way to get it done on my own, and if I do, it's really, really, really, really minor, like a sentence that I just change around.
>
> —Michael, age fourteen

## The Ethics Gap

Before moving on, it's worth considering the idea of ethics and discussions about ethics in schools. Too often, perhaps, teachers assume that
students share their values or should. Plagiarism, in particular, is treated
as a moral offense by many educators. Perhaps it is in its most egregious
forms, but in cases of unintentional misunderstanding of the rules of collaboration, or even in terms of understanding the nature of intellectual
property on the Internet, it's important to remember that students may
view the world differently than we do; we may even view the world differently from one another. Rules about collaboration, after all, aren't
established moral laws; they're shared assumptions about what's appropriate and what's not.

Students who regularly download material from the Internet, who
believe that because the material is free it can't be protected by law, or
who have just grown up in the Wikipedia era of pooling information
may have a completely different view of what constitutes appropriate use

> You can lead a dis-
> cussion about pla-
> giarism in your
> classes using the
> discussion ques-
> tions in the *Plagia-
> rism* Study Guide
> available online at
> www.heinemann
> .com/gilmore.

### Voices from the Classroom

The most bizarre case of plagiarism I experienced involved an Asian student whose parents were hardworking immigrants. I caught the student using direct quotes from a Kenneth Burke essay on Shakespeare that he had accessed on the Internet. When the student showed no guilt about direct plagiarism in our conversation, I asked for a conference with the parents in guidance. The father paid good money for the computer and felt that any material his son got from its use was rightfully his. The affair was a communication fiasco. It was never fully resolved. The student rewrote the paper paraphrasing Burke, giving him credit in the context of the paper.

*—High school teacher*

than faculty do. Add to that mix the difficulties of being a foreign student whose culture treats plagiarism differently—some students in such a situation feel at a loss to understand the moral rules being thrust upon them. One study revealed that international students who feel the pressures of language barriers, time constraints, and culturally relative understanding of conventions and emphases are more at risk for plagiarism (Gourlay 2006, 8).

Understanding that an ethics gap exists is the first step to discussing it with students, and that discussion in turn may lead to a better understanding of why plagiarism occurs. Plagiarism *does* still occur, though, no matter how well you understand the reasons. The next chapter is about dealing with those inevitable cases as they become apparent. Yet it's always a good idea to be prepared, to know how and why, before actually wading into confrontations (especially for those of us who are conflict sensitive). Reasons don't excuse, but they do matter.

## Works Cited

CBS. 2002. "Cheating in the Heartland?" *48 Hours*, May 31. www.cbsnews.com/stories/2002/05/31/48hours/main510772.shtml (accessed Feb. 20, 2008).

Goldberg, Carey. 2006. "Have You Ever Plagiarized? If So, You're in Good Company." *Boston Globe*, May 1. www.boston.com/news/globe/health_science/articles/2006/05/01/have_you_ever_plagiarized_if_so_youre_in_good_company/?page=1 (accessed Feb. 22, 2008).

Gourlay, Lesley. 2006. "Negotiating Boundaries: Student Perceptions, Academic Integrity and the Co-Construction of Academic Literacies." Internet Plagiarism Advisory Service. 1st International Plagiarism Conference. www.jiscpas.ac.uk/documents/papers/2006Papers08.doc (accessed Mar. 24, 2008).

Harris, William. 2007. "Plagiarism in Academe." Middlebury College. http://community.middlebury.edu/~harris/plagiarism.html (accessed Feb. 20, 2008).

Howard, Rebecca M. 1999. *Standing in the Shadow of Giants: Plagiarists, Authors, Collaborators*. Stamford, CT: Ablex.

# 4 *Reducing the Sentence*

## *How We Respond to Plagiarism*

Pop quiz:

You catch a student plagiarizing. There's no doubt; the student has copied an entire paragraph of an essay from an online source. What do you do? Fail the student? Make the student rewrite the paper? Turn the case over to the administration at your school? Ignore it and hope the problem goes away?

Even when teachers do deal with cases of confirmed plagiarism, they often do so quietly, keeping the matter private between instructor and student. According to a 2007 study by Sandra Nagelson published in the journal *Plagiarism*:

- Teachers of undergraduates "deal with" about 38 percent of suspected plagiarism cases.

- When teachers do pursue cases of plagiarism, over half discuss the rules of citation with students and 48 percent use "informal counseling" methods.

Such statistics speak volumes about what concerns teachers—namely, student well-being, learning, and reputation. They may also reflect many teachers' natural aversion to dealing with misconduct. Did I enter the profession, they think, to talk about the big ideas of human knowledge or to give kids demerits?

Some would argue, however, that informal counseling and discussions let students off the hook. "It's like a speeder getting a warning instead of a ticket," one of my peers said to me. "That's fine, unless the guy's getting pulled over every day by a different cop. Then he's just getting away with it and never making any corrections." Few would argue against a need for both informal and formal discipline at the middle and high school levels in general, but some would suggest that there may be

## TOP TEN: Reasons Plagiarism Goes Unaddressed

1. Teachers want to maintain an atmosphere of trust.
2. Teachers lack confidence in administration to follow through with consequences.
3. Teachers suspect plagiarism but have no hard evidence to support those suspicions.
4. Instructors make assumptions about student knowledge of citation rules and procedures.
5. Teachers feel consequences may follow a report but fear the severity of those consequences and the effect on students.
6. The prevalence of an "I don't know how to teach this stuff" attitude regarding attribution results in unreported plagiarism.
7. Unsure of student intent, teachers handle plagiarism internally.
8. The hassle factor makes it easier to ignore plagiarism than to deal with it.
9. The excuse that "it's just a minor assignment" makes it easier to overlook suspected plagiarism.
10. Teachers feel overwhelmed by work, the process, the emotional drain, and the potential fallout from getting involved; in large part, they feel they just don't have the time.

times when informality in discipline enables rather than serves the student. Take, for instance, a case made by one professor in an article titled "Dealing with Plagiarists," in which the author speculates on the frequency of ignoring plagiarism at the college level:

> If each of us were to forgive our students their plagiarism offenses, and give them a second chance, this meant that it was theoretically possible—for a student taking a normal course load—to plagiarize, get caught, and get a second chance 40 different times: once in each course she took in her college career. (Lang 2002)

Lang, who starts his article with a quiz not unlike the one I used to start this chapter (I didn't plagiarize, I promise—coincidences happen!), eventually comes to the same two conclusions most of us who study cases of plagiarism reach: we need to develop fair models of response and to pay more attention to prevention.

Prevention is covered in the second half of this book. First, though, comes the issue of response. What to do? Is there a correct answer to our pop quiz? If there is, finding it unfortunately won't be as easy as choosing one answer from a multiple-choice list, nor will we ever be guaranteed to get it right every time. But mustering some information about when and why we should respond may lead us toward a greater understanding of our options for punishment and correction.

## Bucking the System: What Happens When Teachers Are Reluctant to Act?

As with so much of the material written about plagiarism, studies that look at the number of teachers who report cases of plagiarism focus mainly on the world of higher education. A few notable examples:

- At Napier University in Edinburgh, United Kingdom, the 63 percent of professors who fail to report plagiarism derive their reluctance from "the time it takes to deal with cases of academic misconduct" (Read 2006).

- In a study reported in the journal *Ethics and Behavior*, college faculty members "overwhelmingly agreed that dealing with instances of academic dishonesty was among the most onerous aspects of their profession" (Keith-Speigel et al. 1998).

- Other studies found that professors in the first two years of their career were "most likely to confront students they suspected of cheating" (Valparaiso University 2006).

Unfortunately, with so little hard evidence about middle and high school practice, it's more difficult to reach definitive conclusions, but based on the anecdotal material I gathered I'm led to believe the following:

- the majority of middle and high school teachers deal with cases of plagiarism in an informal manner;

- few middle and high schools have written plagiarism policies with clearly defined consequences—most cases are left to the discretion of individual teachers and administrators; and

- middle and high school students cheat as much as, if not more than, college students.

## My School, My Classroom

I asked students at my school how they thought teachers *do* and *should* respond to cases of plagiarism. The majority of students answered that teachers *do*

- handle plagiarism internally by simply warning students and/or assigning a grade of zero in 55 percent of cases
- turn in plagiarists 37 percent of the time
- rarely ignore the offense entirely (8 percent of cases)

The same students suggested that teachers *should*

- require students to rewrite the assignment only (29 percent)
- require a rewrite and report the incident (25 percent)
- simply give the student no credit (27 percent)
- give the student no credit and report the incident (19 percent)

A full list of questions to prompt faculty discussions about plagiarism is available in the online Study Guide at www.heinemann.com/gilmore.

One conclusion that follows from these assumptions is that while middle and high school teachers may respond to cases of plagiarism more often than college teachers, they don't necessarily do so consistently and may be *more* reluctant to use official channels. It's also worth noting that the wide variety of assignments and the sheer number of papers with which many teachers deal (think of 150 students multiplied by several written assignments each week) make detection a Herculean task.

Given that one goal of many middle and high school teachers may be to teach students how not to plagiarize before those students enter a one-strike collegiate system, a focus on informal procedures may not be all that bad. Many teachers don't want to be locked into a rigid, punitive system that allows little room for variation in cases; at the same time, a lack of such systems may give students the impression of a random, arbitrary environment in terms of response. The ideal system, then, for a middle or high school would promote a sense of equity and at the same time allow students to move along a reasonable learning curve based on any number of factors involved in cases of plagiarism: grade level, the nature of the assignment, the frequency of offenses, and the reasons behind the occurrence, for instance.

Achieving such a system may rank among the toughest accomplishments for any school—right up there with keeping the photocopier stocked with paper or keeping the morning announcements from eating away at class time. In order to make it work, teachers must actually detect plagiarism first and then act, in some manner at least, when cases occur. What's more, teacher reaction can't occur entirely in confidential meetings and arrangements, but at the same time policies can't enforce such strict, irreversible punishments that teachers will avoid them altogether.

We'll get to overall school policy in a moment, but first, let's consider individual classroom policy and how a single teacher might work to turn the tables on reluctance to act.

## Teaching Opportunities

Any classroom teacher confronted with a case of plagiarism will either be grateful for a written policy or wish she had one, but only if the policy allows some flexibility. Putting dire consequences in writing may feel good on the first day of the year, but you'll regret it when you find you've placed yourself in a position that affords no compromise. Nonetheless, the first rule of responding to plagiarism must be to *set clear expectations and define your options for response.*

Note the difference between defining your options and defining your response. I encourage you to build some latitude into a classroom policy—not so much latitude that your students will see you as wishy-washy, unfair, or arbitrary, but enough that you can consider cause and effect in dealing with individual students.

Therefore, in constructing a personal plan for responding to plagiarism, I suggest you think about the following.

### CONSIDER A TWO-STRIKE SYSTEM

James Lang, whose article on plagiarism I quoted earlier, suggests having students sign a form after a first offense that goes

> ### Voices from the Classroom
>
> I learned the definition of plagiarism in fifth grade. The piece I produced was six pages long; it was a work I now shudder to read, but it was a creation of my own imagination. Several days after turning my story in, I was called out of science class by my English teacher. She held the pages of my story in one hand and a pen in the other. She selected a circled word from one of the sheets; "Josephine, what does *cerulean* mean?" Flustered and confused, I blanked on the denotation but eventually muttered that cerulean is a shade of blue. The teacher laid my story on the desk, looked me right in the eye, and asked me with every nuance of accusation, "Josephine, do you know what plagiarism is? It's when you use work that is not your own and claim it for yourself. Now, tell me the truth—is this story your own creation?"
>
> "Yes," I replied, appalled by the question I had just been asked. Unsatisfied, my teacher wrote a lengthy letter on the last page of my story, "reminding" me of the definition and severity of committing plagiarism.
>
> —*Josephine, age sixteen*

on file in case a second offense occurs. If you choose to use such a form (you'll find an example in Figure 4.1), be sure to follow these steps:

- Get an administrator's approval first—having your principal on your side from the beginning will make any formal procedures much easier later on.

- Attach a copy of the written assignment and hard evidence of plagiarism to the form itself.

- Counsel the student in person, explaining the problem and attempting to discover the reasons for the attribution problem.

- Have both the student and the student's parent sign the form, if possible. Have a backup plan, such as involving administration, if the student or the parent does not wish to sign the form.

Such a form will benefit you most if the penalty you assess in the first instance is not so severe that the student's record is permanently damaged by it (I prefer having students rewrite the assignment to failing them in the first instance), but such considerations must be measured against the student's grade level and past history. A second-semester senior who turns in a downloaded paper is quite a different case from a seventh grader who cuts and pastes a few lines. It's also worth exploring the possibility of filing such forms as a department or school so that students won't plagiarize in multiple classes without correction.

### Discuss the Escalation of Consequences as Students Age
In the interest of time, I often spend a few minutes summarizing the contents of honor codes and consequences from a few institutions. It would be ideal, however, to have students research other systems themselves and develop a class chart that portrays the consequences for plagiarism. When I discuss the escalation of consequences with students and teachers, I share a model of common consequences that looks like the one in Figure 4.2.

Not every case will follow this progression, of course, and this model pertains mainly to first offenses and assumes that most cases involving younger students are unintentional. If you've spent days going over citation format with a class of ninth graders, it's certainly reasonable to factor citation into a grading rubric, while older students who make genuine and relatively minor mistakes might deserve counseling and a second chance before failing a major assignment. The idea of such a discussion, however, is to demonstrate to students that the time to learn appropriate models of attribution is the present—there are plenty of examples to be

# Attribution Awareness Form

Student Name: _____

Teacher and Course Name: _____

Date: _____

Assignment: _____


Description of attribution issues with this assignment:

_____

_____

_____

_____

_____


Description of correction plan:

_____

_____

_____

_____

_____


*By signing below, I agree that there were problems with my attribution of source material on this assignment and I agree to follow the correction plan above. I understand that plagiarism or failure to cite sources in the future may result in more severe penalties such as failing grades or disciplinary measures. I also understand that I am not required to sign this form.*

_____          _____
Student signature                                              Date

*Figure 4.1*

| Grade Level | Consequences of Plagiarism |
|---|---|
| below 6th grade | discussion, correction |
| 6–8 | correction, rewriting |
| 9–10 | correction, rewriting, grade penalties |
| 11–12 | rewriting, failure on the assignment |
| college undergraduate | rewriting, failure (assignment or course), expulsion |
| graduate student | expulsion |
| professional | loss of job/contract, legal penalties, loss of professional reputation |

*Figure 4.2*

found of the dire results brought upon themselves by those who failed to learn that lesson.

### FIND OUT WHY

Before you take any action, give the student a chance to explain. If nothing else, this will give everyone time to consider an appropriate and ethical response.

### SAVE EXAMPLES TO SHARE, BUT DON'T IDENTIFY STUDENTS

You would never, of course, wish to betray the confidence and privacy of students by parading their mistakes in front of their peers, probably even anonymously. At the same time, students benefit from seeing and discussing the processes of other students. I save (as anonymous papers) examples of heavily plagiarized material as well as more minor infractions to share with students in later years. I often have students track down citations and phrases within the papers of previous students—not only do students see how quickly some plagiarized material can be found, but they also follow reproducible routes that lead them to legitimate, reputable sources.

## A Discipline Problem: The Options for Dealing with Plagiarism

Because so much research on plagiarism is focused on higher education, the study of possible responses to plagiarism is unfortunately limited; not only do professors have a different range of possibilities (how many teachers at the graduate level, for instance, can keep a kid after school or have regular chats with their students' parents?), but they may also have a different view of their classroom role. In his book *Teaching with Integrity,* Bruce Mcfarlane notes of college professors that "many regard themselves, first and foremost, as researchers or experts in a disciplinary or professional field rather than *teachers* of their subject" (2004, 8). While it's true, as well, that high school teachers more often claim an interest in a subject area as a motivation for entering the profession than do elementary teachers (who cite their love of working with children more often), nevertheless the desire to educate adolescents in skill areas as well as content areas is generally shared by most middle and secondary teachers.

In other words, the question that a middle or high school teacher may ask is not, what punishment does this student deserve? but how can I help this student learn not to make this mistake in the future? Fairness plays a role in punitive decisions; consequence may be part of helping a student learn; consistency of policy matters, but the fundamental desire to help the student can change the nature of deliberations about how such consequences and policies play out.

Take, for instance, the case of biology teacher Christine Pelton, which I described in the last chapter. Pelton had students and parents sign a contract early in the year which included an antiplagiarism clause. When some sophomores used cut-and-paste plagiarism to complete Pelton's leaf project assignment, she issued failing grades. Though she was supported by administrators in her school, the school board later reduced the value of the assignment from 50 percent of the semester grade to 30 percent, ensuring that some students didn't fail the course.

> **Voices from the Classroom**
>
> My philosophy is that consistency is best; inconsistency creates a problem within the community and it begins to erode what you're trying to do and combat. Teachers and administration need a common sense of what to do; all cases need to be reported to me or to an honor council, just so that it's a matter of record and so that we can work with the student fairly and democratically. That creates a level playing field between students, too. Some teachers handle situations internally thinking they're doing what's best for the child, but it comes back to bite them *and* the child. Even when it's unintentional, if due process still happens, it becomes a teachable moment—the student knows he or she came to the precipice, but it doesn't have to go further. That's a better learning situation; I know from my time in the classroom that when you try to handle things individually, sometimes you don't get the learning you thought you would or wanted to have.
>
> —*High school principal*

The case is often reported as a travesty of school board administration, and I certainly believe that the board's decision undermined Pelton's authority in the classroom. "Pelton resigned in protest in an episode that some say reflects a national decline in integrity," stated an AP report featured on CNN (CNN.com 2002). But I've always been plagued by questions that weren't asked by the media in this case. Any assignment worth *50 percent* of a semester grade must take a good deal of class time. Did Pelton discuss plagiarism with her classes during that time? Was the weight of the assignment in concert with the effort required to complete it? Was outright failure (CNN noted that Pelton's principal and superintendent agreed that "it was plagiarism and the students should get a zero for the assignment," and the school board did not change the zeros, only the weight they carried in the course) the best and most appropriate response?

The answers to these questions may be yes, and even an answer of no doesn't change the debatable nature of the school board's decision. But the fact that reports of the incident didn't ask these questions suggests to me that we're missing something in our discussion of responses to plagiarism. The automatic assumption that students who cut and pasted material in a major assignment deserved, in essence, to fail a required course doesn't strike me as taking into account the responsibility of the school to educate as well as discipline. The AP-CNN article focused on the "tolerance of dishonesty" displayed by the school board, but I have to wonder whether intolerance of dishonesty should be equated with severity of response.

What *are* the possibilities, then, for responding to cases of plagiarism in middle and secondary school classrooms?

### FAILING THE ASSIGNMENT

Pros? A score of zero on the assignment sends a clear message to the student committing the infraction and to others. Failure is also quite often the result of plagiarism at the college level, and students should be aware of that fact. Cons? Well, let's consider. To begin with, failure on the assignment assumes intent and rules out any pretense of education or correction as a necessary and valuable step (unless it's accompanied by a

---

### Voices from the Classroom

At the beginning of the year in seventh grade, we see a lot of unintentional plagiarism. "I didn't understand that when you said research you didn't mean just go get some information online." It's also, though, the first time kids are asked to think abstractly and to apply knowledge at this level, so it's hard to combine that with citation and research practice. But fairness is important and right and wrong are important to sixth graders, so sometimes they tend not to cheat as much on purpose as older students might. We handle those cases on the first go-around internally, and after that we go through the formal process.

—*Middle school teacher*

command to rewrite). A failing grade also assumes that the amount of plagiarism in the assignment overshadows any and all original work in the same paper and, in some cases, in the course (since failing one assignment can, in many cases, lead to failing an entire class). And that's just making an F; what about making a zero? In the case of Pelton's students, the principal and superintendent reportedly supported assigning zeros for 50 percent of a semester grade, but the gap between the highest and lowest failing grade is usually around sixty or seventy points. Should every case of plagiarism automatically cause a teacher to leap over that gap entirely?

I don't wish to make the case, either, that students should *never* fail an assignment for plagiarism. A student who copies, say, all three sentences of a three-sentence homework assignment probably deserves no credit. A student who downloads an entire paper may also deserve such penalties. But for those who mistakenly paraphrase poorly or who cut and paste a small percentage of a paper or who do some, but not all, of their own work, I'd urge consideration, at least, of a middle ground. As educator Douglas B. Reeves (2004) put it, "To insist on the use of a zero on a 100-point scale is to assert that work that is not turned in deserves a penalty that is many times more severe than that assessed for work that is done wretchedly and is worth a D." The argument against a zero—a score that can cripple a student's overall grade—but in favor of a higher mark that still represents failure applies as equally to some cases of plagiarism as it does to work that is not turned in at all.

> ## Voices from the Classroom
>
> In eighth grade, I was an A student, but I hated my English teacher; the homework seemed dull and pointless. The assignment was to write summaries of each chapter; no analysis, just summary for the sole express point of making sure we read the book. I decided I could outsmart the system. I went to a lesser-known website and turned in the chapter summaries completely plagiarized. About halfway through *To Kill a Mockingbird*, the teacher caught me and another student who had decided to cheat in the same way.
>
> I was totally embarrassed, and still deeply regret my decision to plagiarize. However, I view that day as a turning point in my academic career; I started to work harder and have never *really* plagiarized again (apart from minor offenses from copying textbook material). I feel my decision to cheat was not because I lacked moral judgment or because I was not aware of what I was doing. I viewed the assignment as busywork and above all else, the teacher failed to reward individual students who put effort into the assignment, which eliminated the incentive to work harder to get a better grade. . . . I think that if the school had decided to punish me more, the real reason not to cheat would have been lost to me. It would turn an offense that is illegal because it is stealing into an offense that is wrong only if you are caught by your school.
>
> —*Andrew, age seventeen*

## REWRITING THE ASSIGNMENT

Obviously, the most valuable exercise for student learning is to correct mistakes in some fashion and, thus, learn not to repeat them. Many teachers include some form of rewriting in their response to plagiarism, especially in a first instance and with younger students. Others worry about the message that might be sent to other students, who could come away with the idea that the consequences for plagiarizing aren't really that bad—if you get away with it, great, and if not, then heck, you just do the assignment after all.

One might consider, too, the possibility of consequences other than grades combined with rewriting. Such cases might work in much the same way many teachers deal with students who don't turn in an assignment at all; rather than simply receiving a zero, the student loses social and extracurricular privileges (break or recess time, study halls, freedoms during the lunch hour, attendance at assemblies, or after-school club and sport practices and meetings) until the work is completed. The difficulty with such a system, and even with rewriting in general, is that it places a burden on the teacher as much as on the student—the teacher loses time and must manage late and rewritten papers. That sacrifice of a teacher's time makes it difficult to create schoolwide policies that use this sort of enforcement, though individual teachers may wish to pursue such systems within their own classrooms.

### Failing and Rewriting

I know a number of teachers who believe that the natural consequence of turning in unoriginal work (or no work at all) should be to fail and have to complete the work anyway. I've personally never been satisfied with this double-whammy approach; it seems to rob students of motivation for doing the assignment well and replace it with a punitive sense of just getting work done for it to be done. I grant, however, that such approaches may require a consideration of specific teaching disciplines; a math teacher may well need students to complete assignments in order to build a certain skill base, while language arts assignments may be building general skills that can be ascertained from one assignment as much as the next. Nonetheless, I generally view this approach as having more to do with punishment than with learning content and skills.

### Recording the Incident (Using a Two-Strike or Tiered System)

In the online magazine *Suite101*, one author offers, first and foremost, this advice for "college professors, high school teachers, anyone who values teaching" about preventing plagiarism:

> Let students know you mean business. Establish a strict penalty for students who plagiarize. . . . Let them know you have a zero-tolerance policy for cheaters. If someone is caught, do not hesitate in enforcing the policy. (Rockler-Gladen 2006)

There are a lot of zero-tolerance policies out there; a quick search for the phrase "zero tolerance plagiarism policy" on Google yields page after page of syllabi and honor codes that seem to take Rockler-Gladen's advice to heart.

Here, on the other hand, is what Russell J. Skiba at the Indiana Education Policy Center concluded in a major study of zero-tolerance disciplinary policies in schools:

> The appropriate application of consequences at opportune moments is certainly one tool for teaching students that actions have consequences in a lawful society. Yet it is clear that the school punishments that are central to zero tolerance policies have not been studied enough to determine whether they yield benefits sufficient to outweigh the well-documented and troubling side-effects. (2006, 14–15)

Skiba is focusing on policies involving drugs and weapons for the most part, but his conclusions, I believe, are no less applicable to cases of academic dishonesty. What are the side effects of a zero-tolerance policy for plagiarism in middle and high school? The student faces the possibility of failure without hope for recovery, disengagement from the class and from school, alienation from the teacher and the administration, and a general feeling of unfairness about who gets caught and why; the teacher, on the other hand, may be stuck with an antagonistic, apathetic, and disengaged student for the rest of the year. More to the point, the unfortunate side effects for the teacher may extend beyond the immediate case; after all, a zero-tolerance policy implies that the student is entirely responsible and may allay any concerns about the perceived or real value of assignments or education about plagiarism in the classroom.

A two-strike system may provide a balancing point for teachers wishing to maintain an emphasis on student responsibility without enforcing consequences that may cancel out student learning. Ideally, such a system would involve schoolwide participation; in such a system, the first instance of plagiarism noted by any teacher is duly recorded, while the second instance, whether caught by the same teacher or another one, leads to consequences. Enforcing such a system on a classroom-by-classroom basis does, admittedly, provide the possibility that students escape serious response in class after class, but I think it's more likely that middle and high school students will learn from mistakes over the course of a year if they're taught how and why they should avoid those mistakes.

The key to such a system, however, is communication. A teacher who notes plagiarism in one instance but never communicates with students, parents, or administrators might as well have ignored the problem entirely.

### REQUIRING SOURCE MATERIAL ON FUTURE ASSIGNMENTS

A colleague of mine who gives daily reading quizzes never has students who miss class make up the quiz; instead, he counts the next quiz double. It's not a system that works for everyone, but in some cases of poor paraphrasing and unintentional plagiarism, one might consider a similar approach: "I'll grade this assignment without any penalties, but for next week's paper you have to include source material even though nobody else in the class does." There are drawbacks to such an approach, including the possibility that a student might feel he has gotten away with something, but one major benefit for the teacher is that the student is warned, the skills are reinforced, but there are no extra papers or post-deadline assignments to grade.

## Involving Parents and Administrators

A few years ago, I sat in a parent conference and listened as a student's mother proudly explained to me the process she and her son used to complete his essays. First he would make an outline and collect the evidence, then they would discuss it together, then he would write a rough draft, and then she would type the draft for him.

"When you type the paper," I asked, "do you make corrections for him?"

"I don't change anything major," she said. "I just correct spelling and syntax and grammar."

A little more probing revealed that the mother, a college professor, had designed for her son a template for his essays that followed the five-paragraph model to a T, sentence by sentence. As the five-paragraph essay was exactly what I was trying to get students *not* to write in twelfth-grade English, I recognized that communication was going to be an ongoing issue in this case. I also recognized, however, that this mother was one who cared deeply about her son's education, who wanted him to learn and do well in school, who was willing to talk with me openly and frankly about her involvement, and who was, in many ways, working against all that I was trying to accomplish in the classroom, albeit unintentionally.

Had I used the word *plagiarism* to describe her son's papers, I have no doubt that the conference would have taken a wildly different turn—I'd

> ### Voices from the Classroom
>
> As a counselor, I talk to kids about plagiarism. Usually it comes up because there's already been some disciplinary action—somebody's gotten caught. It's different for different kids, but you try to clarify values. When students actually stop and think about the values they have and the values they want to be known for, cheating seems different to them. But information is so differently accessed these days that many students don't take the time to stop and think about values, to ask themselves, "Am I doing something wrong?"
>
> —*High school counselor*

have faced a defensive and intractable mother rather than one who was listening to what I had to say. At the same time, how could I allow a college-bound senior to have his papers partially written and almost entirely formulated by someone else? How would he learn independence of thought and skill?

I left that conference ready to research and implement a plan for communicating with parents the need to set an example for students, to show them that doing their own work came with its own rewards. My subsequent research, however, revealed a disturbing trend: more and more, authors and teachers seem to view parents as the enemy. Professionals seem to sense that parents will either serve as an obstacle to prosecuting cases of plagiarism or as coconspirators in the crime.

To be fair, there's reason for concern about parent involvement. Every year I talk to parents about the college essays their sons and daughters compose, and I'm aware of the painful truthfulness to reports that such essays increasingly show a level of parent involvement that other teachers at my school complain about mainly during the science fair. As the *Boston Globe* reported,

> With the scramble to get into elite colleges at a fever pitch and with a rising number of educational consultants and college essay specialists ready to give students a competitive edge, admissions officers are keeping a sharp lookout for essays that might have had an undue adult influence. In some admissions offices, such submissions receive the dubious distinction DDI, short for "Daddy Did It." . . . The concern over heavy-handed adult involvement is mounting as the admissions essay has become a pivotal part of the application, a key way for students to stand out from the throngs of applicants with top grades and SAT scores. (Schworm 2008)

For students (and parents) confronting the college application process, the stakes are high and getting higher. That very fact may increase the feeling among parents that their help is needed not just on the application essay but also on ordinary assignments throughout the school year. Every English or social studies teacher I know has run across the paper that just sounds too good not because it was downloaded from the Internet but because a parent or tutor offered excessive help.

For the same reason—because the stakes are high—parents who would never condone cheating in theory, when backed into a corner by sudden accusations of plagiarism leveled at their children and by the possibility of failing grades, may vigorously defend a student in a meeting with teachers after the fact. Such conflicts, in turn, place administrators in the difficult position of backing either the teacher or the parent, with little room for mediation or conciliation.

Prevention and preparation are as important in dealing with parents and administrators as they are in combating student cheating. As you plan possible responses and policies concerning plagiarism, consider some of the following ideas.

### MAKE PARENTS PARTNERS

Educate parents early about the dangers of plagiarism. Warning parents in a course syllabus or letter about plagiarism is fine practice, but only if the parents share the teacher's understanding of the causes, manifestations, and policies regarding academic dishonesty. Consider sending parents not just your written policy but also handouts or web addresses that demonstrate the problems some students have with cutting and pasting, citation, and paraphrasing. You might even demonstrate at a back-to-school night or through written correspondence proper and improper Internet sources, search techniques, and attribution.

### HELP PARENTS LEARN HOW TO HELP THEIR CHILDREN

We want parents to help their children with learning, but how much help is too much? Here, too, teachers have the opportunity to make parents partners or obstacles. A few suggestions:

- Be clear about your expectations of parental involvement in written and other assignments. Emphasize mainly how parents can legitimately and productively help children with homework, but give a few examples of how a parent might cross the line with too much assistance.

- Give parents some pointers for checking reading and writing. Suggest, first, that they remember that writing is hard and that students need affirmation as much as proofreading and editing. Advise, too, that parents concern themselves with asking questions, and mainly questions about content, rather than correcting student work.

- Note that both the teacher and parents are responsible for navigating students through a system that involves consequences for dishonesty. While we hope parents will encourage original work, we too add to the high-stakes atmosphere; even if we do so for legitimate reasons, we need to be aware of the need for increased information and preventative steps on the front end so that parents don't feel ambushed by accusations when it's too late for them to help.

### De-Emphasize Extrinsic Awards; Emphasize Intrinsic Rewards

In the journal *ScienceDaily*, Eric M. Anderman noted that "it is ironic that many students view the reward for doing well in the classroom as being able to get out of additional learning activities" (APA 1998). Such a comment on classroom culture should serve as a wake-up call to teachers who inadvertently promote a focus on reward rather than learning, but it should also be communicated to parents. Unfortunately, parents often feel that their power over their children's schooling (after all, they're not actually there with them, are they?) comes to them in the form of what they can give or take away in the evenings or on weekends.

The intrinsic rewards of learning for families, of course, are hard to quantify; they frequently occur during dinner conversations and rides in the car. Teachers can promote such conversations, however. Consider, for instance, the power of a quick email or phone message that, instead of reporting a grade, simply suggests that a mother talk to her daughter about a recent essay not because the grade was high but because the subject was just plain interesting. Consider an assignment that requires a high school boy to ask his parents for their views on an issue, not their proofreading skills. Many parents want to be involved in the education of their children but don't know how to do so except to react to report cards and parent conferences. ("I was never good at that Shakespeare stuff," they'll say. "And calculus? Forget about it.") Teachers who give parents accessible entry points into the educational process not only help those families share the intrinsic rewards of education but also help create parents who are involved in the class enough to understand assignments and expectations and thus help prevent the need for cheating in the first place.

### Clearly Align Your Policy with School Policy

You don't want to get into any situation where your personal classroom policy is at odds with school policy, and be careful about a more stringent set of expectations and consequences than your school administration is prepared to back up.

### Establish a Train of Communication Before You Need It

It's not a bad idea to deal with plagiarism issues quickly, but not so quickly that you leave anyone out of the loop. When dealing with formal plagiarism procedures, I suggest giving the student a chance to explain her case to you in writing, then talking to an administrator, then immediately contacting parents. No principal wants to be blindsided by a phone call from an aggravated parent; you're more likely to gather support if you move quickly to inform all parties.

### KEEP A PAPER TRAIL

Hold on to everything—the original assignment and student product, copies of the source material, written student explanations, emails or records of phone calls to parents. Arrange all relevant papers chronologically and make copies for parents before entering into any conferences on the subject of plagiarism.

### FOCUS DISCUSSIONS ON LEARNING, NOT PUNISHMENT

If and when you do contact parents about cases of academic dishonesty, make sure to show your (genuine) concern for a student's learning and achievement. Emphasize the skills you are teaching, not the crime. Keep your own emotions in check to show that there's nothing personal about a student's offense; it's another step, rather, in that student's educational process.

As with all responses to plagiarism, teachers need to remember that parents and administrators can be allies in the effort to educate students rather than merely punish them. When we ignore cheating or fail to use all of the resources at our disposal to help students because it's a hassle for us to pursue such options, we not only do a disservice to the one student who fails to learn from his mistakes but also to the many others who may see such a negative model and take the wrong message from it. Cases of plagiarism must be dealt with, but as the remainder of this book suggests, it's better to try to avoid them altogether. Teachers can learn from plagiarism, too, and those lessons are what the next three chapters will explore.

## Works Cited

American Psychological Association (APA). 1998. "Research Shows Homework Does Boost Academic Achievement; but Overemphasizing Grades and Performance May Lead to Cheating." *ScienceDaily,* Mar. 4. www.sciencedaily .com/releases/1998/03/980304073520.htm (accessed Feb. 25, 2008).

CNN.com. 2002. "Teacher Resigns Over Plagiarism Fight." Feb. 7. http:// cnnstudentnews.cnn.com/2002/fyi/teachers.ednews/02/07/plagiarism .dispute.ap/index.html (accessed Feb. 26, 2008).

Keith-Speigel, Patricia, Jennifer Washburn, Bernard E. Whitely Jr., and Barbara G. Tabachnick. 1998. "Why Professors Ignore Cheating: Opinions of a National Sample of Psychology Instructors." *Ethics and Behavior* 8: 215–27. www.leaonline.com/doi/abs/10.1207/s15327019eb0803_3 (accessed Feb. 23, 2008).

Lang, James M. 2002. "Dealing with Plagiarists." *Chronicle of Higher Education.* http://chronicle.com/jobs/2002/05/2002051401c.htm (accessed Feb. 23, 2008).

Mcfarlane, Bruce. 2004. *Teaching with Integrity: The Ethics of Higher Education Practice.* London: RoutledgeFalmer.

Nagelson, Sandra. 2007. "Academic Misconduct by University Students: Faculty Perceptions and Responses." Plagiary: Cross-Disciplinary Studies in Plagiarism, Fabrication, and Falsification. 1:1–10.

Read, Brock. 2006. "Professors Aren't Policing Plagiarism." *Chronicle of Higher Education.* http://chronicle.com/wiredcampus/article/1360/professors_arent_policing_plagiarism (accessed Feb. 23, 2008).

Reeves, Douglas B. 2004. "The Case Against the Zero." *Phi Delta Kappan*: 324–25.

Rockler-Gladen, Naomi. 2006. "How to Prevent Plagiarism." *Suite101.com.* http://collegeuniversity.suite101.com/article.cfm/how_to_prevent_plagiarism (accessed Feb. 27, 2008).

Schworm, Peter. 2008. "College Applications Can Be Too Good." *Boston Globe*, Feb. 12. www.boston.com/news/education/higher/articles/2008/02/12/college_applications_can_be_too_good/ (accessed Feb. 25, 2008).

Skiba, Russell J. 2006. *Zero Tolerance, Zero Evidence: An Analysis of School Disciplinary Practice.* Bloomington Indiana Education Policy Center, Indiana University.

Valparaiso University. 2006. "Valparaiso University Honor System." Oct. 26. www.valpo.edu/student/honor/CAI.html (accessed Feb. 23, 2008).

# 5 Acting, Not Reacting

## Giving Students the Tools to Avoid Plagiarism

There's no doubt that if we want to prevent plagiarism, not just police it, we need to address causes. Remember the metaphor from the introduction? Instead of performing triage—bandaging the worst wounds and cutting out infections—we need to work harder on keeping the injuries at bay in the first place.

The question is, how far back before cases happen do we reach in our efforts to stop academic dishonesty? Is a good classroom policy enough? How about redesigning our assignments? What about revisiting our expectations of what student learning looks like entirely? Heck, what about reconsidering the very nature of our competition-driven education system and the high-stakes environment in which many students are placed?

On the one hand, I admit that cheating in general and plagiarism specifically are symptoms of much larger health issues that schools face today, symptoms that stem from the mixed message we send when we talk about learning and achievement as if they're synonymous while demonstrating through our practices that they're not. Imagine telling a basketball player that it's not about winning or losing but how you play the game one day and that she'll be cut from the team if she doesn't score thirty points the next—or, to use a metaphor closer to home, imagine telling a classroom teacher that his goal is to instill creativity, imagination, and higher-order thinking, then basing his pay entirely on the standardized test scores of his students. The town crier for reform in this area on a national level is Alfie Kohn, who frequently argues against the competitive environment of schools by speaking out against grades and rankings:

> Grades, however, are just the most common manifestation of a broader tendency on the part of schools to value product more than process, results more than discovery, achievement more than learning. . . . The goal of acing a test, getting a good mark, making the honor roll, or

## TOP TEN: Methods for Plagiarism Proofing the Classroom—The Student Perspective

I asked the students in my school to describe assignments made by teachers that deter or eliminate plagiarism either purposefully or accidentally. I've compiled their suggestions into ten categories. These students recommend that teachers

1. explicitly discuss the rules, expectations, and parameters of assignments (including attribution) when the assignment is made;

2. make assignments that focus on thinking and learning rather than recalling data;

3. give students choices (of reading, topic, or assignment format) to increase interest;

4. consider assignments and assessments that involve technology, presentations, performance, and writing in combination;

5. include group work and discussion as a step in the assignment process;

6. involve classes in discussions of grading scales and weights before assignments are given (and make choices about grading policies that reflect those discussions);

7. be fair, supportive, and respectful of students;

8. avoid busywork assignments and worksheets;

9. create a class environment in which students aren't compelled to cheat by peer pressure (e.g., don't have students sit too close to one another during tests); and

10. use class time to help students with assignments in ways that will make plagiarism unlikely or less necessary.

impressing the teacher is completely different from—indeed, antithetical to—the goal of figuring out what makes some objects float and some sink or why the character in that play we just read is so indecisive. (2007)

If we follow Kohn's argument, we might envision an educational environment in which students are motivated not by report cards but by assignments, teachers, projects, and a general atmosphere that encourages learning for its own sake.

And yet, we do live in a competitive environment—basketball teams want to win and teachers *are* evaluated based partly on test scores, whether we like it or not—and real teachers exist in real classrooms, where the rules of the entire game aren't easily changed and where students and parents don't easily break away from a system in which they've operated throughout their lives. If challenging the commonly accepted values that lead to plagiarism policies (such as the concept that copying is an absolute wrong in all circumstances) is tough, then challenging the value system embodied by letters on a report card is a task akin to battling windmills with a paper clip. The idyllic learning environment evoked by Kohn's argument might work well in kindergarten, many teachers would argue, but in a calculus class, where learning is tough work? Forget about it.

Nonetheless, Kohn's point sticks: the article I quoted earlier ends by reminding us that "how we educate students is the dog; cheating is just the tail." This chapter and the next two, then, focus on how we educate, not just on how we respond to cheating. The argument that underlies these chapters runs like this:

1. Students need the academic tools that will help them not to cheat (an understanding of the rules of attribution, digital literacy skills, and research tools).

2. When teachers help students take ownership of assignments rather than be owned by them, plagiarism is less likely to occur (how we design assignments matters).

3. School culture—and classroom culture—can promote plagiarism or work to prevent it (both explicitly and implicitly).

Or, in simpler terms, what you can do to prevent plagiarism is teach the right skills, design the right assignments, and create the right atmosphere. Neglect those areas, and you resign yourself either to ignoring plagiarism or to spending your time angrily rooting out and punishing offenders.

This chapter addresses the first part of my argument, while the next two chapters address points 2 and 3. What follows, I hope, are methods that will help you prepare students in ways that will make plagiarism less frequent and less necessary for students in your own classes.

## Out of Cite: Teaching Attribution

No matter which citation method your school uses—mine uses MLA, but many teachers use APA (American Psychological Association), Turabian, or a host of others—there are three questions a student might ask about citing sources within a paper: How? When? And, of course, why?

I've noticed that research assignments tend to focus on the first of these questions far more than on the last, yet the first is probably the easiest to answer. MLA, for instance, provides specific instructions for citing just about every source, all of which are based on the simple premise that in-text citations need to point clearly to bibliographical entries (which in turn point clearly to the original sources). If, for instance, I note that the author of *Writing Research Papers: A Complete Guide* advises students to avoid plagiarism by developing "personal notes full of [their] own ideas on a topic" that "synthesize the ideas of the authorities" (Lester 118), then it's fairly simple to figure out from information in the same source that I *must* include the name of the author and page number on which the information can be found in my parenthetical note (as I've done) and that the parentheses should immediately follow the quotation (which they do). If I'm unsure about the format of the parenthetical citation or the bibliography entry that must accompany my quotation, I can find a model quickly and with little fuss at numerous online sites such as Easybib.com and Citationmachine.net.

> ### Voices from the Classroom
>
> When we change works, from a novel to a play or from Faulkner to Shakespeare, I remind them about citation format. Most of them know how to do basic citation, but reminders are useful. I say it as though I assume they know *why*: "Of course you know that it's important to cite." If I feel we need to go deeper than that, we can. We also talk about why we use our citation method as opposed to other methods. For students who have trouble writing anyway, it's a longer process and you complicate it by using different citation methods, which puts them more at risk for plagiarism, but for better students, they balance those different types and get ready for college. It's a trade-off, I suppose.
>
> —*Tenth-grade teacher*

In other words: the *how* is the easiest part of the equation. Sure, there are occasional sources that throw students (and me) for a loop—how to cite a text by one author that is quoted in an appendix by another that is included in an online version of an anthology, for instance (*that* formatting rule I'd have to look up carefully)—but in general, citation and bibliography formatting are the easy part. So why are students reluctant to do it? Some possible answers:

- When we ask students to cite, we ask them to interrupt what is fundamentally a creative process of composition with a menial and noncreative task.

- If a student perceives that citation is difficult (or doesn't have any knowledge of appropriate citation procedure), she is more likely to avoid the exercise altogether.

- If citation seems to have no importance other than as a part of an eventual grade, a student's motivation for citing correctly will naturally be low.

- Some students fear that citing sources will make their work seem less original.

Yet many teachers address citation issues mainly by distributing to students examples (or directing them to an online site that shows examples) of proper citation for the style used in the course. That's not bad practice—students need clear guides, and many easily understandable guides of this sort exist. But a handout is not sufficient here; it doesn't clearly answer the when? or why? questions that the reasons for avoiding plagiarism I mentioned previously embody. I can play a simple scale on the piano all day long, but unless someone tells me why that exercise is valuable and when I might use the skill, I'll go watch *American Idol* instead.

By all means, either teach students how to cite correctly or give them the resources to find out for themselves. About once a semester, I distribute a paragraph and about four or five example sentences that refer to it (one with the author's name mentioned in the sentence, one without, one that uses enough text to offset as a block quotation, one that quotes a word in the middle of a sentence, etc.) and let students figure out the citation format for themselves, after which we go over examples together. Many students actually appreciate this exercise; they want to get it right in their papers.

No matter how many times you conduct such an exercise, though, you'll still see papers where citation format is incorrect or missing altogether. That's because without an appreciation of the value of attribution, students will never fully buy into the need for it at all.

### *Timing is Everything: Teaching Students* When *to Cite (and* How)

Let's face it; if you're going to write a book about plagiarism and originality, you've got to be pretty darn careful to get your source material correct. I've tried hard to do that in this book, but it's no small challenge. When I write, sometimes I work on a computer at school, sometimes at home, and most often at the local coffee shop (people ask me how in the world I can work in public like that, but compared with the environment created by the two kids I have at home or the one created by the two hundred at school, a coffee shop is a blissful oasis). I don't use note cards; I keep track of URLs, titles, and authors in a spreadsheet file. My school librarian helps me obtain books, but I do use a lot of Internet sources.

While writing this book, I often worked on multiple chapters at once—*and* this wasn't the only piece I was writing at the time.

No, I'm not trying to elicit tears on my behalf—I'm just making the point that if I've worked harder than ever to be sure my source material is correct and still struggled with the simple *logistics* of it all, imagine the feelings my students have when compiling a major research paper, with sources they've grabbed from three different libraries and six different computers. How do they keep track? In the simplest terms, I want them to construct the following for themselves, as I have:

1. a system and routine for keeping track of source material;

2. an internal sense of when to cite (based on the rules of the appropriate citation format);

3. a knowledge of basic citation rules, with the ability to unearth the complicated ones as necessary; and

4. an understanding of the ethics of attribution.

My colleagues in middle school have the same goals, but they play out differently. An eighth-grade teacher I know has every student, every year, complete one hundred note cards that look just like those I created when *I* was in eighth grade; the college-bound seniors in my class, I believe, need more flexibility to create a self-sustainable system. I require MLA citation; our history department requires the same students to use Turabian. The eleventh-grade teacher across the hall has strict rules for students about using block or offset quotations (no more than two per essay); I encourage students to use such quotations in a more organic fashion, as necessary. It's OK for these differences to exist, as long as they're discussed with students and the reason for the differences is made clear (the eighth-grade teacher, for instance, is introducing the concept of attribution for the first time; I'm not).

> **Voices from the Classroom**
>
> I cannot say how many people have explained to me what plagiarism is and what it is not, or how many different versions I've heard. They all say plagiarism is using someone's ideas without giving them credit. Then why have teachers said if you list a source in the bibliography and don't cite it internally that you are plagiarizing? The source is in the works cited; you've given it credit. . . . The problem lies in the fact that everyone has a different set of rules for plagiarism. This is frustrating, confusing, and leads to accidental plagiarism.
>
> —*Allison, age sixteen*

The three following sections cover note taking (system), decisions about when and how to cite (the internal sense), and citation format. As you read them, consider the importance of student understanding at every stage of the research process.

TAKE NOTE: PREPARING THE WAY FOR CITATION

The simple fact of the matter is that most teachers instruct students to take research notes as they themselves were taught to take research notes. I've seen dozens and dozens of graphic organizers for note taking in class, while reading, and during discussions, many of which are valuable, but for the most part, ask a veteran teacher how to take notes for a research project and he will likely answer, "Note cards." There's a good reason for this, too: note cards worked for many generations of students and teachers. Those teachers who continue to use them mean to offer their students a system for capturing vital information about a source. Consider the two examples of the traditional note card from a real tenth grader's research paper on the poet Elizabeth Bishop in Figure 5.1.

Though particulars vary, the form of these note cards, dictated by the student's teacher, more or less reflects the traditional manner of taking notes: one card contains a single piece of information with a link to the

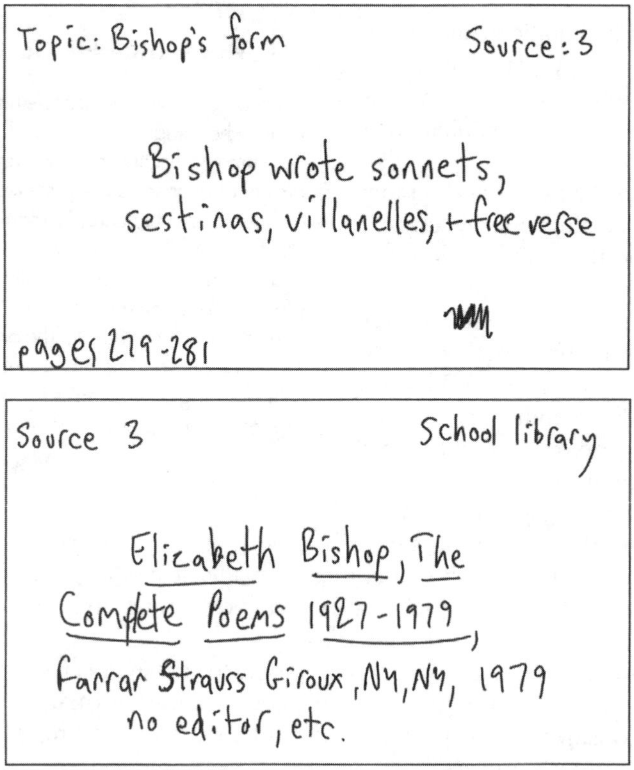

*Figure 5.1*

## YOU NEED TO KNOW: Do Teachers Cheat, Too?

According to a survey of teachers conducted by Teachnet.com (Engel n.d.):

- 57 percent of teachers cheated when they were students
- 12 percent of teachers have helped students cheat on a standardized test
- 74 percent of teachers feel that the pressure of standardized testing makes it more likely that teachers will cheat
- 11 percent of teachers say that cheating by teachers is sometimes justified
- 30 percent of teachers state that parents of students accused of cheating are likely to be angry at the teacher
- 12 percent of teachers think that there are some cases in which cheating by students is acceptable

If you're comfortable enough with your students, it might be interesting to have a conversation with them about the temptations to cheat for professional educators and other kinds of professionals. What pressures exist that might tempt teachers themselves, even those who fervently oppose plagiarism, to cheat?

source card; the second contains the necessary information to format a bibliographical entry for the source. Most teachers who require note cards have students collect their notes on multiple cards, then arrange them according to an outline and use them to compose the final paper.

I'm not out to bash teachers who still require note cards, and I've heard some reasonable defenses of the practice (first and foremost, note cards pretty clearly demonstrate to students exactly what information is required to cite properly). At the same time, I recall my own friend in ninth grade, who fabricated *every* note card for a paper that required us to compile more than one hundred of them. There was little chance the teacher would catch him at the time—the Internet didn't exist and we were allowed to visit the public library to collect sources, so tracking down the sources themselves would have required considerable effort.

To many of today's students, note cards seem as quaint as vinyl records. I showed the note cards from Figure 5.1 to a class of high school seniors who were currently working on thirty-page literary analysis papers. All twenty students had completed significant research for the paper without any particular guidance from their teacher as to the form their notes must take; of the twenty, none had used note cards like those I showed them, at least not since middle school. So how did they take notes? By

- bookmarking websites in their Internet browsers
- printing or photocopying source material
- keeping a list of URLs in Word or Excel, with annotations
- making notes on electronic sticky notes (notes that appeared on their computers' desktops) using a free program
- remembering and making note of the keywords they used to search for material online
- returning to the online catalog of libraries, from which they could access all information about their sources
- saving files from electronic journal collections such as JSTOR or Questia.com
- simply inserting quotations as they wrote the paper using a cut-and-paste method and immediately entering bibliographic material into a saved file on a site such as Easybib.com

One girl I spoke to just laughed when I asked her whether note cards wouldn't be a more certain system. "Do I look like I *want* to waste my time handwriting all that information and then retyping it when I can do it with about two clicks?" she asked. But what about the possibilities for shuffling and reorganizing notes? She shrugged. "What do you think a mouse is for?"

Whole books could be written about note taking, but for our purposes, let's refocus on a single objective: we want students to take good notes while researching so that they won't plagiarize. I'd contend that requiring note cards, unless you're going to (1) have students make them before your eyes or (2) hunt down all of the sources in your spare time, may well have the effect of increasing plagiarism. I'd also recognize, however, that students need to be taught systems. Here, then, are two mnemonics I recommend to students as alternative methods to help make notes more effective and to deter plagiarism:

### CAPITAL IDEA

The unfortunate part of this anagram is that the letters don't fall absolutely in order of importance, but they are all intended to remind students of important pieces of information—the pieces they'll likely need before using the source in a paper.  The full version:

**C**ity—the city where the work was published (if a print source)

**A**uthor of the work

**P**age—page number or specific part of a site where the information can be found

**I**nformation—the salient quotation, fact, or idea that will be used by the student

**T**itle—again, of a print source or web page (for magazines and journals, this includes volume and edition number)

**A**nnotation—personal notes about the source, its usefulness, and how it might help the student

**L**ocation—where was the source found?  In a library, at a URL?

**I**nternet Host—or publisher of a print source

**D**ate—when was the source published or last updated?

**E**dition—or volume number of a journal or magazine

**A**ccess—the date on which a website was accessed

Some sources, of course, require a slightly different approach (a speech or interview, for instance). Some might not require all of this information. Note, too, that this mnemonic leans toward Internet usage, but it includes the information most often needed to cite print sources, as well.

The second mnemonic:

## CHoMP

The CHoMP note-taking strategy was published in the *English Journal* by Kathleen Guinee and Maya B. Eagleton, who described it as "one solution for teaching students to transform information into knowledge" and as a response to "an alarming number of students" who "unwittingly plagiarize large portions of their final research products" (2006, 46). The simple version:

**C**ross out small words, such as prepositions and conjunctions.

**H**ighlight important information in the remaining text.

**M**ake Notes based on the highlighted information by abbreviating, truncating, making lists, using symbols, and drawing instead of writing full sentences.

**P**ut the notes into your own words.

As a sample, Figure 5.2 contains a passage from Guinee and Eagleton's original article with steps 1 and 2, crossing out and highlighting, completed.

Step 3, note making, might look like Figure 5.3.

And step 4, rewriting, might look like Figure 5.4.

As an introductory approach to note taking, I find CHoMP quite helpful. Eventually, of course, the object should be to move students past such step-by-step approaches, which slow down the research process in the interest of careful attention to originality. In order to do that, students must internalize the note-taking process more and more as they mature; CHoMP is a good first step in that direction.

Based on our research experiences, we think the CHoMP strategy has promise for helping students to paraphrase source documents and avoid plagiarism in their research projects. However, students still need literacy foundations and additional strategies for producing high-quality research products. (51)

*Figure 5.2*

PROMISE
PARAPHRASE
NO PLAG.
←→
STILL NEED
LITERACY FOUND.
MORE STRATEGIES

*Figure 5.3*

The CHoMP strategy, its authors assert, might help students paraphrase and keep from plagiarizing, but those same authors recognize the need for other approaches to research and writing for most students.

*Figure 5.4*

## A Fine Balance: How Much, How Often, from How Many Sources?

Most teachers have an instinctive feel for the number of sources, quotations, and citations a paper requires just as they can sense the amount of time left in a class period or when it's going to rain based on the behavior of kids. Students, however, often don't have a clue about this information. It's easy to forget that those of us who read student work on a constant basis understand the construction of papers more clearly than do students who may have written only two or three research-based products—if that—in their lifetimes. Some guidelines, therefore, may be in order.

Yet research is, or should be, an organic process, like word length or sentence variety. To mandate strict figures is to run the risk of stifling creativity and originality of voice as much as making work easier. The answer we'd *like* to give to the question "How many sources should I use?" is, of course, "As many as you need" (substitute *pages* or *cups of coffee* or *camels* for the word *sources* and, depending on the task at hand, the answer is just as tempting). At least as a starting place, students might reasonably ask for more direction. I start by describing a basic pyramid structure for papers (see Figure 5.5), in which every important point is supported by at least two sources or quotations; the structure works whether one is writing a two-page essay on *Julius Caesar* or a five-page research paper on Caesar's conquest of Gaul.

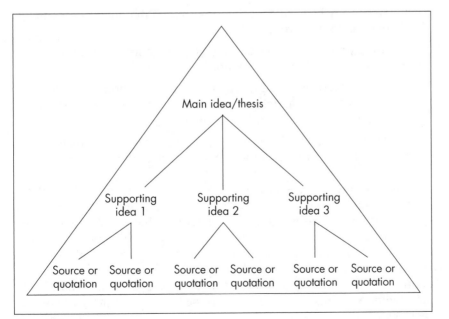

*Figure 5.5*

One can also imagine expanding this model indefinitely by adding more supporting ideas or dividing supporting ideas into even smaller units of support; one could also, for good measure, increase the number of sources or quotations necessary to support each point.

It's not an organic process of research, but it's a place to begin. Other general guidelines you might consider:

- one source overall for each page of a research paper (e.g., a five-page paper requires at least five sources)
- at least two citations for each page of a research paper (e.g., a five-page paper requires at least ten citations)

Again, such guidelines are only meant as introductory strategies to move toward a principled decision about proof and citation. I also have students describe to a partner their answers to the following questions about a single section of a research paper or project:

- Have I included enough evidence to support my points?
- Have I cited all of the sources that deserve credit for the ideas I've presented?
- Are my sources varied, reputable, and balanced?
- Would a reader see a trend in my sources that might raise questions about my process?
- Are my sources evenly distributed throughout the section? If not, is there a valid reason why not?
- Have I clearly and sufficiently explained the quotations and sources I used, including establishing a context for each source's authenticity or relationship to the topic?
- Are there types of sources (or specific sources) that a reader would expect to see in my paper that aren't there?

Only through discussion, reflection, and modeling will students eventually reach a level of comfort with the use of sources and research that makes the process natural and ordinary; at that point, strictures and guidelines can be eased and modified to allow the integrity of the student's work to guide the number and location of pieces of evidence. Remember that the ultimate goal, as with so much in teaching, is to render the teacher-created assignment and its rules unnecessary and in their place equip students with the skills needed to set and achieve goals of their own design.

### A Method in the Madness: Teaching Citation Format

Let's say you want to quote this sentence in your research paper. What information would you include in your citation? It depends on the format (see Figure 5.6).

Figure 5.6 shows the simplest format: citing the source at the end of the sentence. But now imagine the variations on citing the sentence using MLA format alone:

- One writer asks us to imagine quoting "this sentence in your research paper" (Gilmore 85).

- Gilmore asks us to imagine quoting "this sentence in your research paper" (85).

- Gilmore refers to using his own sentence "in your research paper" (85) at the start of one section of his book.

- Educator Barry Gilmore poses this thought:

  Let's say you want to quote this sentence in your research paper. What information would you include in the paper? (85)

And we've not even discussed the vagaries of bibliographical formats yet. Asking students to juggle these rules in their heads just for the sake of it is akin to trying to teach a dog a dozen tricks at the same time (no, no, I'm not calling the students I teach dogs—that wouldn't be fair to the students *or* the dogs).

There are no clever exercises that are worth the time it takes to make students remember arcane citation formats in and of themselves, especially not when there are a dozen easily accessible web services to do it for them. I recommend providing students a very specific style sheet or

| Format | In-Text Citation | Used Mainly By |
|---|---|---|
| MLA | (Gilmore 85) | English and languages |
| APA or Harvard | (Gilmore, 2008, 85) | social and physical sciences |
| Chicago or Turabian | Footnotes or endnotes | history and related fields |

*Figure 5.6*

online resource to use as reference while they format papers. However, I also recommend that you consider the following possibilities:

- *Explain* why *formatting works as it does, as much as possible.* Ask students why it might be more important to one group of scholars to know the date of a publication than to others. Ask why the period might go after the parentheses when using an in-text citation and before the parentheses when using block quotations.

- *Devote class time to putting in place or double-checking citation format— or make it a specific homework assignment.* One way or another, give students the opportunity to slow down and check the attributions without it interfering with the creative process.

- *Treat citation checking as an aspect of proofreading.* Proofreading a paper should ideally come after major editing and revision takes place; citation format, likewise, requires a checking process that is tedious and necessary but shouldn't distract from an overall reaction to a piece of writing.

- *Recognize the difficult nature of creating some bibliography entries.* Some formatting questions are really tricky. You might even make a game out of trying to uncover the precise formatting for a quirky source. Always remind students, though, of the fundamental goal of citation format: it provides a common means for scholars to track down the sources you use in your research. That goal should always remain in sight.

- *Discuss the ethics of citation regularly.* Don't let a "do this because I said so" attitude prevail or students may begin to inch closer to an attitude of their own: "I don't know why I'm doing this, so I might as well cheat." Encourage originality by keeping students focused on ethics and reasons rather than merely on procedures.

Of course, discussing ethics is all well and good, but only if you're prepared to answer difficult student questions or statements about attribution. The next section deals with those questions.

### The Attribution Solution: Teaching Students Why to Cite

"Why does citation matter?"

The question hangs in the air of my AP class for a few seconds before anyone ventures an answer.

Finally, Rafael raises his hand warily. "Because you'll fail us if we don't do it?"

"OK," I say. "What else?"

Another student, Janet, shrugs. "You've got to say where your sources come from."

"How come?" I ask.

"So someone else can find them, I guess. But I don't think that really matters much in *my* papers. It's just, like, practice."

Janet's got a point, and I don't have a great response handy, because with the particular paper we're discussing, it's not likely anyone else will try to find her sources.

It's worth discussing with students why they should cite sources, but it helps to be armed with an actual list of reasons. Here are a few I offered Janet's class by way of response:

- Plagiarism defeats the main point of writing assignments: learning to think critically and analyze.

- When a student fails to cite, it destroys trust in the academic setting. It's a lot harder to regain trust than it is to lose it.

- Plagiarism and the failure to attribute material cheat the reader; they make it impossible to follow a trail of sources and to track down ideas (teaching students to follow a bibliography to find more sources is a good way to illustrate this point).

- Plagiarism and the failure to cite, of course, have consequences, often punitive, for students who are caught.

- A plagiarized source is often impossible to track down again when the author wants to find more information.

If you want to teach students why to cite, I suggest handing them a paragraph with the citations removed and sending them to track down the sources or to find another source that verifies the information in the paragraph—I'd use, for instance, a nice meaty paragraph about the vestigial body structures of common glass lizards. Set them loose in your school library for a few minutes, then get them back together and show them the original paragraph with citations included. How might having that information have changed their search for verification? How does withholding the bibliography affect their sense of fairness?

Of course, you needn't pull an elaborate trick on students to impress this

> ### Voices from the Classroom
>
> I wrote an essay that summarized what I read in some articles and typed it up and cited the sources on my bibliography page. I thought what I was doing wasn't plagiarism but since I didn't have internal citations, which I didn't know what they were, I lost points for plagiarism. If I would have known about all rules for citations, it would have been avoided.
>
> —*Andy, age seventeen*

lesson—they'll probably get it without even looking for the sources, just by comparing passages. But it helps, too, to give students the sense that someone *might* actually go looking for their sources. Ever since the conversation with Janet's class, each year I collect the research papers students write and post them on a website; I also compile the papers into a photocopied book and file it in our school library. When students choose to write their annual literary analysis papers on a topic similar to one that another student has written about before, I send them to find the paper. I tell them to check the bibliography and see if any of the sources will help. I also make it clear, in this way, that I remember the paper and its argument and will recognize plagiarism in part or wholesale. The lesson is valuable to them for two reasons: on the one hand, it shows students that following a bibliography to find source material is a respectable practice, and on the other, it gives them the sense that a future student might actually come along and read *their* papers—and check their sources. Being a part of an ongoing discussion may be the best reason any student has ever had for getting citations right.

## Team Efforts: Collaboration and Cheating

In 2007, the Duke University school of business expelled, suspended, or failed more than thirty students (around 10 percent of the class of 2008) for cheating. The offense: corroborating on a take-home, open-book exam in violation of the school honor code. *BusinessWeek* (2007) commented on the scandal the next month:

> It's easy to imagine the explanations these MBAs, who are mulling an appeal, might come up with. Teaming up on a take-home exam: That's not academic fraud, it's postmodern learning, wiki style. Text-messaging exam answers or downloading essays onto iPods: That's simply a wise use of technology. . . . That's not to say that university administrators should ignore unethical behavior, if it in fact occurred. But in this wired world, maybe the very notion of what constitutes cheating has to be reevaluated.

And reader backlash against the *BusinessWeek* commentary was predictably full of outrage: cheating is cheating, readers insisted, and no matter how flat the world gets, individual accountability still stands for something.

The Duke case, in which students were, on average, twenty-nine years old and generally experienced in the workplace and in education, raises even more profound questions for middle and high school. Imagine the mixed message a seventh grader might perceive: Cooperation and teamwork are important, but I want to see what you can do on your own.

Contribute to your group, but not too much. There's no excuse for grammatical errors in your essays—didn't you get someone to *proofread*?—but too much help on an essay is plagiarism.

Most classroom teachers balance group work with individual accountability, and most of the time students navigate their teachers' expectations fairly smoothly. Explicit instructions help: "You can work together to compile your notes," a teacher in my school tells students before open-book classroom exams, "but once you walk into the exam, you're on your own." One can imagine, however, the difficulty students might face in some situations. Say, for example, one student calls another with a question about homework—she doesn't understand some of the terms, even though the teacher explained them in class. Is it cheating for her friend to explain? What if it's vocabulary homework? Different teachers might have different answers.

A fallback position for many teachers is that transparency matters: students who collaborate don't try to hide it, while those who cheat do. Many of us have had students show up with answers that were worded identically, or nearly so, and we determined by talking to the authors that they worked together closely. For most of us, that same scenario has also sometimes revealed that one student copied from the other.

Discussion questions for faculty about giving students the tools to avoid plagiarism are available online in the *Plagiarism* Study Guide at www .heinemann.com/ gilmore.

### Teaching Opportunities

There are too many upsides of having students work together for good teachers to insist that students complete all work independently; students benefit from active engagement, hearing points of view other than the teacher's, learning to distribute tasks, navigating the difficulties of interacting with a team. But how to stave off plagiarism? In my own classroom, I use these guidelines in developing group projects:

- *Group work should require and foster interdependence.* Both the assignment and any designated student roles (reporter, researcher, moderator) should encourage all group participants to take an active role in both process and product.

- *Students should have a chance to comment on and receive comments on the group's work as a whole, but allowances should be made for individual performance as well.* I create rubrics (see the next guideline) that include self-evaluation, evaluation by other group members, and my own observations.

- *Groups should be involved in making their own rules.* Before groups begin work on any major projects, I require them to create and sign contracts covering several areas. What factors will be important in my evaluation of their product? How will the group respond to members who don't pull their weight (and how will they be graded)? What happens if the group can't agree? Using these contracts, we create rubrics that will ultimately help me assess the work of the group.

- *Group work should occur in clearly defined steps with explicit instructions about when to work together and when to work independently.* I often have students work together on the first steps of assignments that are traditionally thought of as independent projects—literary essays, tests, even exams.

- *Groups need assistance.* No matter how good the written guidelines, students need a teacher to check in, prompt thinking, and oversee trouble or difficulties in procedure.

These suggestions don't all combat plagiarism directly, but they do contribute to an overall culture of collaboration that goes a long way toward making unintentional plagiarism less likely. They allow for limited interaction (at least), give students a comfort zone and clearly defined expectations for how to interact, and promote the idea that learning and creativity alike occur in multiple stages that alternate between individual thought and application and collaborative learning and discussion.

## A Tangled Web: Digital Literacy

One day in the hall, I overheard a student named Carlos moaning about dinosaurs. From what I could hear, his art teacher was requiring one for a homework assignment.

"She wants you to find dinosaurs?" I asked.

Carlos laughed. "Yeah, Mr. Gilmore, right, I have to bring a stegosaurus to class. Get real. I didn't say *dinosaurs*, I said *dino-source*."

The student Carlos was chatting with let me in on the secret. "He means a book."

Ah. A book. *Dino-source*. As in extinct. The term tells me a great deal about how my students view sources of information and their usefulness.

The Internet is here, for good or ill, and thus for students today, digital literacy is a skill as important as literacy itself. Because of the organic and uncontrolled nature of the Internet, with its unimaginably extensive content, many teachers prefer that students avoid it altogether, while for most students it's a natural first and last step on any quest for information. In the summer of 2007, for instance, I surveyed a group of eighty high school sophomores and juniors from around seventy different Tennessee high schools. I asked those students what kinds of sources they were allowed to use on research papers.

- Seventeen percent of students used online sources only (including print sources accessed online).

- Twenty-five percent of students used print sources only.

- Fifty-eight percent of students used a mix of print and online sources.

Most teachers would agree, I suspect, that the 17 percent of students who used only online sources would be the poorer if they never learned to visit a library and sort through the index of an actual book or to scan the stacks for texts that might be relevant—besides the vast quantity of material that is still inaccessible online, such research takes one in directions that are not reproducible through a Google search. But what about the quarter of all the students surveyed who used *no* online resources? What methods are they missing out on, and what skills are they not developing? What dangers will they face when they do turn to the Web for information in later years?

Consider these scenarios, which are based on real websites:

- An eighth-grade student with a reasonable knowledge of the Internet, assigned to write a paper about Martin Luther King, tries the URL www.martinlutherking.org without even using a search engine. Having done so, she thinks the site is a real find: there's a big portrait of the civil rights hero along with links to pages with titles such as "The King Holiday: Bring the Dream to Life," "Suggested Books: The Life and Works of King," and "Download flyers to pass out at your school." But at the very bottom of the page, in the smallest type on the page, is a link to the site host, named only as Stormfront. The teacher, seeing this source in the student paper, makes a trip to Stormfront's home page and immediately finds more links: a Gospel radio show, a radio address by someone named Don Black, and, in one corner, a logo that starts to raise suspicion—it includes the words "White Pride World Wide." The teacher searches for Stormfront and comes up with a link for Wikipedia's entry on Don Black, Stormfront's webmaster, who, it turns out, is also a Grand Wizard of the Ku Klux Klan and a noted white nationalist—*that's* who has created the original site on King, and the material provided by the original links soon reveals the biases one might expect from such a source.

- A fairly savvy high school junior winds up at the site www .gatt.org. Even to a fairly discerning viewer, this site appears to be a genuine website posted by the World Trade Organization.

Deeper investigation (prompted by articles on the site that call, for instance, for institutionalized slavery in Africa) reveals that the site is maintained by a group called the Yes Men, not the WTO.

- For a health class, a student turns in a paper asserting that the first male pregnancy has been successfully conducted. The proof? A slick website with articles and data and a YouTube documentary that seems pretty darn real. Will students know this is a joke?

There are also, incidentally, some nice hoax sites out there that were designed to demonstrate the dangers of digital illiteracy; try, for instance, searching for "California's Velcro Crop Under Challenge" (http:// home .inreach.com/kumbach/velcro.html), "Save the Pacific Northwest Tree Octopus" (http://zapatopi.net/treeoctopus/), and "Buy an Ancestor Online" (www.fulkerson.org/ancestors/buyanancestor.html). Even these sites could be misleading, but they also make nice tools for teaching digital literacy.

One could take from the existence of bogus websites the lesson that the Internet is a minefield of misinformation to be avoided at all costs, but students won't wish to avoid it, and really, with so much *useful* information available online, why would they? The lesson I prefer is this: if we don't teach our students digital literacy skills, no one will, and they will be that much more likely to fall prey to propaganda and half-truths. Students are warned frequently (though not enough listen) about the existence of sexual predators online, but few of them think of the existence of what I refer to in my classes as values predators—those who seek to mislead and reprogram the minds of web users. Even if one discounts the worst misleading sites, there are so many kinds of bad research to be conducted on the Web. There are sites posted by amateurs, sites that are biased, sites that are outdated.

Students need strategies for smart web use; if we are going to ask students not to plagiarize, we must make sure they feel confident and comfortable conducting research online. Here are some suggestions for helping them gain those strategies.

### Start Your Engines: Searching for Information Online

Type the word *plagiarism* into Google and the first two sites the search engine returns are Plagiarism.org, a site maintained by the same company that owns Turnitin.com, and Wikipedia's entry on *plagiarism*. Type the word into Google Scholar and the first site returned is a chapter of an online book titled "Borrowing Others' Words: Text, Ownership, Memory, and Plagiarism," by Alastair Pennycook; you can read some, but not all, of this chapter in the online version.

Many students don't know that most search engines offer both a basic method of searching and multiple ways of narrowing a search for information. It's common, now, to search for images or videos, but how often do students use a Yahoo! product search, Google's U.S. government search engine, or an AltaVista search using a specific date range? Most search engines offer numerous ways of narrowing a search; Google Scholar, for instance, which limits results to a broad range of academic abstracts, journal articles, theses, books, and similar sites, is accessed simply by clicking on the menu labeled "more" at the top of the Google home page.

Students who know a few basic search commands also navigate the sea of information online more readily. A few examples can be found in Figure 5.7 (which also, not surprisingly, led me to the discovery that very little has been posted online about the role of monkeys in cases of plagiarism).

| You type this . . . | The search engine looks for sites that . . . |
|---|---|
| plagiarism monkeys | mention plagiarism and monkeys in any way |
| plagiarism and monkeys | contain information about *both* plagiarism and monkeys |
| plagiarism and not monkeys | contain information about plagiarism but not about monkeys |
| plagiarism or monkeys | contain information about either plagiarism or monkeys |
| "plagiarism and monkeys" | use the exact phrase "plagiarism and monkeys" at some point |
| +title "plagiarism" and monkeys | are titled "Plagiarism" and contain some mention of monkeys |
| domain:edu and plagiarism and monkeys | are hosted by a domain ending in .edu (or whatever domain you specify) and include information about plagiarism and monkeys |

*Figure 5.7*

Narrowing the options of a search is a useful trick for students, but you should also discuss with them the arbitrary nature of such engines. Pages are ranked by search engines in a variety of ways; the information for which a student is searching doesn't always come up in the first ten hits out of six hundred thousand. Smart searching means trying a number of different phrasings, key words, and search options; it also means taking the time to follow links and delve into web content in more than a cursory manner.

## SEARCH

I wouldn't actually let students loose on the Internet armed with nothing but a vague topic such as "plagiarism" or "monkeys" any more than I'd send my six-year-old daughter into a candy store with a thousand dollars—not, at least, without giving those students a system that promotes self-regulation and critical thinking. One strategy I share with students (I model a search for them in class using an LCD projector and my computer) uses the acronym SEARCH: search, examine, assemble, return, collect, harvest. Here are the steps:

*Search for a topic using an advanced search engine (such as Google Scholar).* Sometimes students like to start with a general search using a search engine or Wikipedia to familiarize themselves with a topic. That's fine, but when it's time to find usable source material, I encourage students to begin with a narrow search that will yield not just immediate information but bibliographic links and reputable sources right off the bat.

*Examine reputable sources and follow links to major journal archives and other sources, for instance:*

- JSTOR
- Questia
- Enotes
- Google books
- Amazon book previews
- ERIC
- Findarticles.com

Many of the articles one finds through an advanced search are archived through online sites that require registration. However, one can often access a preview, abstract, or excerpt, and often enough the full text is available as well. Students can make a note of promising articles that are not easily accessible for later reference.

*Assemble a source list from bibliographies, notes, and references.* One of the most valuable lessons students can learn is how to follow the trail of a bibliography—note the sources one writer uses, look those sources up, and then check each bibliography for other sources that might also be useful.

*Return to a search engine to look for specific items.* Having found a potentially useful title in a bibliography, it's often worthwhile simply to cut and paste that title into a search engine and run a broad search for an online text. Often, for instance, the author of an article will post a copy on a personal website.

*Collect more search keywords (and more sources).* The process can be repeated, but along the way students will probably learn more ways to narrow the search. A student might begin research by typing the term *plagiarism* or *cheating* into the search engine, for instance, but as he investigates phrases like *academic dishonesty*, names like McCabe and Howard, and potential sources such as the *Chronicle of Higher Education* will come up again and again; the student, noting these recurring terms, can then refine his search accordingly.

*Harvest an original bibliography of reputable sources (and go to the library!).* A student who goes online or to a library armed with a list of titles is far ahead of the game; eventually, this process of checking and rechecking keywords and bibliographies and of using a variety of search options will result in a useful bibliography.

## CARS
On his website, Virtualsalt.com, author Robert Harris (2007) offers this quick reference guide students might use to evaluate Internet resources. The acronym CARS makes it easy for students to remember.

*Credibility—author's credentials, evidence of quality control.* Indicators of lack of credibility: anonymous sites, lack of contradictory points of view, bad grammar.

*Accuracy—timeliness, comprehensiveness, audience awareness.* Indicators of lack of accuracy: out-of-date, incomplete, or overly general information, information that can't be corroborated from other sources.

*Reasonableness—fairness, objectivity.* Indicators of lack of reasonableness: clear biases, slanted tone, conflicts of interest.

*Support—documentation, external objectivity.* Indicators of lack of support: no references to sources or other sites, no contact information or "about us" page, no citations.

I speak to my students frequently about the need not just for useful sources but for reputable ones—Wikipedia, for instance, useful as it is, contains plenty of misinformation (I recently noticed that the article on my own school listed the president of the United States and Michael Jackson as alumni; neither is true). Though I don't tell students never to visit Wikipedia, I also encourage them not to rely on it as a source; it may guide their research but not act as research in its own right. Harris' mnemonic is a useful guide for students in choosing which websites they should or shouldn't include in their own bibliographies.

### Credit Reports: Teaching Students to Check Sources and Citations

No matter how frequently you speak to students about the importance of using creditable sources, they'll need reminding. As a refresher, or for younger students who may need more specific direction, try a source-by-source approach to checking the validity of online material. I call these exercises credit reports. Following are two particular approaches.

#### SELF-ANALYSIS

The handout in Figure 5.8 offers a quick means for students to verify each source they use to complete a research assignment. For some sources (an article from the *New York Times*, for instance), students and I can practically stipulate that the source is credible, but the form still provides a valuable record. For other sites (something like, say, www.teacherswhohatedaffodils .com), the credit report provides students a way to self-analyze sources and report that analysis by submitting the handout for each source with a final draft. The practice of backtracking mentioned on the report merely involves shortening a URL to find the home page or source; a student of mine recently cited information on Iranian women from a web address two lines long, but when she shortened the URL to its most basic form, the information, it turned out, came from a student group whose mission was to support certain political candidates, leading our class to a lengthy discussion about source analysis.

#### PEER ANALYSIS

For major research papers and projects, I often have students trade bibliographies and hunt down one another's sources. I might have them use the same handout for this exercise as for self-analysis; at other times, I might simply have them tag any sites they feel are suspicious (or can't locate altogether). I also ask for volunteers to share with the class sources used by a peer that were particularly successful or interesting in order to validate good research and provide models for other students.

# Student Credit Report—Internet Source

Student Name: _____

Name of Site: _____

URL: _____

Who is the host organization?

_____

When was the site last updated?

_____

How did you find this source? Describe the search that led you to it.

_____

_____

_____

Checklist for finding site host:

- ☐ Shorten the URL (backtracking).
- ☐ Follow links (check bottom of web page/"about us").
- ☐ Do an independent search of any organization mentioned on the site.

How sure are you that this is a reputable source? On what evidence do you base your conclusion?

_____

_____

_____

What's your estimation of the bias of the source? Have you checked links, references, footnotes, or other organizations mentioned on the site?

_____

_____

_____

*Figure 5.8*

## The Culture of the Classroom

Chapter 7 of this book deals with the culture of schools, but individual classrooms have cultures, too. They're created by the bond between teachers and students, the rules and expectations teachers communicate, and how teachers approach their craft—how they teach, for instance, aspects of learning such as attribution, group work, and digital literacy. A healthy classroom culture, I believe, also instills a sense of ownership in students, gives them the feeling that help is available, and focuses on their learning; it also asks students to comment on and change the culture of the classroom itself.

In that sense, nothing can be more important in combating plagiarism than student buy-in. If students understand assignments, assessments, and guidelines, they'll be likely to complete their work more easily; if they help *create* those materials and structures, they're far more likely to pursue originality in their execution of them. Students who discuss plagiarism understand it better; students who discuss plagiarism with a teacher, especially in an open and nonhostile manner, are less likely, I think, to plagiarize.

The next chapter of this book deals with creating assignments and assessments. I encourage you, as you consider your policies and as you read the next chapter, to consider how your own classroom environment serves to combat plagiarism not only through identification and consequence but also through its culture—how you teach, how your students learn, and how you communicate with one another about teaching and learning. Such reflection, ultimately, is the best defense against academic dishonesty of all sorts.

> ### Voices from the Classroom
>
> If you don't draw attention to it, the kids won't think anything about going and plagiarizing. But if you teach *not* to plagiarize and show them how to quote and cite, it's no big deal to simply give credit where credit is due, and it's all well and good. You also show them how easy it is these days—just hop onto Easybib.com or some other site as you go, plug in your sources, and it gives you your bibliography, no big deal. They're more likely to plagiarize, for me, on a poetry assignment or something than on research.
>
> —*Ninth-grade teacher*

## Works Cited

*Business Week*. 2007. "Cheating—or Postmodern Learning?" May 14. www .businessweek.com/magazine/content/07_20/b4034056.htm (accessed Mar. 23, 2008).

Engel, Sally. n.d. "Cheating in Our Schools (Survey Results)." *Teachnet.com*. www.teachnet.com/speakout/survey/cheating.html (accessed Mar. 23, 2008).

Guinee, Kathleen, and Maya B. Eagleton. 2006. "Spinning Straw into Gold: Transforming Information into Knowledge During Web-Based Research." *English Journal* 95: 46–52.

Harris, Robert. 2007. "Evaluating Internet Research Sources." Virtualsalt. June 15. www.virtualsalt.com/evalu8it.htm (accessed Mar. 23, 2008).

Kohn, Alfie. 2007. "Who's Cheating Whom?" *Phi Delta Kappan.* www.alfiekohn.org/teaching/cheating.htm (accessed Mar. 23, 2008).

Lester, James D. 2004. *Writing Research Papers: a Complete Guide.* New York: Longman.

# 6 *Copy That!*

## *Designing Assignments and Assessments*

In my first year of teaching, I assigned each student a poem to research. I thought it was a pretty good assignment; every poem described a specific historical or literary event that provided an avenue for research that could be added to an analysis of the poem itself. In order to minimize complaints (or heck, maybe just to maximize work), I took the students to the library for several days, where they worked diligently and then turned in first drafts.

My brows first furrowed upon reading several pages of clearly plagiarized information about Renaissance London in a paper on Hardy's "Channel Firing"—apparently, the great fire of 1666 was all the student could find in the encyclopedia. Next, I read a lengthy report about Ireland in the early twentieth century from the girl who confused Joyce's *Ulysses* with Tennyson's poem of the same name. The coup de grace? Page upon page of material copied straight out of a reference book first on the Roman poet Horace and then on various other topics beginning with the letter *h* (the student had just started writing and not bothered to stop between entries), all in response to the last line of Owen's "Dulce et Decorum Est."

Rookie mistakes, right? I made a lot of assumptions about what my students knew about research and writing and even more about what they'd *want* to know and how they'd get there. That same assignment—there was no specific prompt other than "analyze this poem and provide research on the content"—would lead, today, to papers straight off the Internet. It would probably also lead to very little learning.

But that doesn't mean that students are incapable of understanding or unwilling to understand these great poems, and I haven't given up wanting to help students see why the poems are great. Some of my colleagues, however, think I'm nuts to assign a research paper on a poem like "Channel Firing." That's just *daring* students to plagiarize, they'd say, and some students agree. If you want to stem the tide of copied papers,

### TOP TEN: Ways to Encourage Originality During the Writing Process

1.  *Specify the sources.* Teach students to research using projects or longer, step-by-step writing processes; for some shorter papers, provide articles or other source material for students and have them quote, cite, and respond to others' arguments using those specific sources.

2.  *Require source proof.* Just having students bring in a source doesn't accomplish much, but requiring visible proof of notes written onto copies of a source can help students in the research process as well as stem plagiarism.

3.  *Build collaboration into the process.* Besides the example I offer in this chapter for developing topics, consider having students collaborate in finding research materials, setting assignment parameters such as length and point of view, or establishing comparisons between works.

4.  *Color code sentences by type.* This is especially easy with typed papers: have students highlight, in different colors, those sentences that are purely original, those that paraphrase other sources, and those that quote. The results will serve as a visual key to the balance of research and original thought.

5.  *Specify an audience.* Keep in mind that critical reviews, journal articles, research proposals, websites, and newspaper features all have slightly different audiences; discussing with students how to write for such audiences not only tweaks papers in a way that may discourage copying, but is also good preparation for a variety of future writing assignments.

6.  *Readjust the stakes.* All things being equal, if an essay is worth half of a final grade, the chances of plagiarism go up. Breaking up the process and increasing a sense of ownership can help, of course, but ask yourself about pressures you're placing on students, and balance the complexity of assignments (not just the time they take) with their weighted value.

7.  *Require specific components.* Specifying a number of quotations, a variety of sentence types, or a number of paragraphs can be both educational and restricting, so be careful about your requirements and how you discuss them with students.

*continued*

> These requirements may also help break up grades for rubrics or scoring guides.
>
> 8. *Involve peer editing.* Even if you don't feel that peer editing always works neatly as a revision tool, there's value in having students share ideas and approaches, and sharing with peers can make plagiarism a less palatable or necessary course of action.
>
> 9. *Break the process into pieces.* Requiring papers to be turned in piece by piece not only keeps students from copying entire chunks but helps them keep their progress under control.
>
> 10. *Require current sources.* The newer the sources, the less likely they are to show up in prefabricated essays.

the argument might go, you have to change the way you make the assignment.

I'm not so sure.

I bristle a little every time I see these common pieces of advice leading off articles about plagiarism—and they crop up so frequently in such pieces that I'm not even bothering to cite a particular source here. The advice:

- assign only very specific topics that make plagiarism impossible;

- assign papers that compare great works to very modern, obscure, or unlikely other works; and

- make assignments personal and creative.

None of this is bad advice in and of itself. I have no problem with giving students specific instructions, with encouraging literary connections that take students in unexpected directions, or with personal, creative writing. In fact, I make all three of these types of assignments pretty regularly. But I do it because it leads pedagogically where I want to go, not because it discourages plagiarism. My middle school colleagues tend, for instance, to make personal and creative assignments routinely, for very good reasons.

My problem is this: does the prevalence of such advice—given as it is with the presupposition that any teacher who doesn't follow it is just *asking* for students to plagiarize—mean that no student will ever again write an original thought about "Channel Firing"? Some would argue that the poem's been analyzed to death already; what new could be said about it, anyway? I'd argue, in return, that if we don't ask students to write about it, we'll never know. Not that I'm so attached to Hardy's poetry, but you get the idea. It's true, too, of a history teacher asking students to write about the Civil War or a science teacher assigning homework about the evolution of sterilization; the history teacher could ask students to compose a piece in which they imagine themselves to be Union soldiers, and the science teacher could have students compare the development of sterilization procedures to the development of something unexpected—say, the Chia Pet—but is either of those topics certain to head students toward the type of learning the teacher would ideally like to see?

> **Voices from the Classroom**
>
> I try really hard to give them topics that I weave together that they might not find online in a way that encourages simple downloading. So if I ask them to compare Kafka and Goethe, they might go and get information about Kafka from one source and they might get information about Goethe from another, but they won't find an essay out there.
>
> —*Tenth-grade teacher*

Before turning too cynical, however, I decided to test out the previous advice. A ninth-grade class in my school was studying the classic Vonnegut short story "Harrison Bergeron," which seemed to me a fairly common text that wasn't as obviously going to lead to essays as, say, a Shakespearian play. So I gave the ninth graders a challenge: I dared them, literally, to plagiarize. I came up with essay topics on the story that followed the standard advice, wrote them on the board, and told the class, "I want you to try to find a paper that would fit this topic online. If you can't, I want to know how hard it would be cobble together an essay without writing much, if anything, on your own."

Then I had them turn on their computers and go.

Let me say, up front, that with that particular class the exercise led to a pretty intense conversation about how and why students plagiarize. I wasn't trying to equip the students to cheat, of course, but to build toward a discussion of the ethics and logistics of cheating. In the short term, though, the activity proved my point (see Figure 6.1 for the results). The bottom line? None of the prompts I developed would keep a determined ninth grader from plagiarizing, and in fact, the more I worked to tweak the prompt, the less likely it became that I'd receive an essay that I could prove was plagiarized. Sure, I could go for the even more specific, the even less likely comparison, but do I really want to grade ninety-five freshman-level essays comparing "Harrison Bergeron" to a song lyric by the rock band Barenaked Ladies, as one of my colleagues suggested?

| Sample Assignment | Sample Student Response |
|---|---|
| *Basic Prompt* | |
| Write a three- to five-page full, formal essay in which you discuss the role of government in "Harrison Bergeron." | It took me about ten seconds to find a free essay online, but it wasn't very good. I could have paid $6.95 for a better one, though—probably worth it. |
| *Using Specificity* | |
| Choose three characters from the story "Harrison Bergeron" and find two quotations from each character. Using those six quotations, write an essay in which you compare the motivations and choices of the three characters. | What a pain, I have to cut and paste those quotations into an essay that I found online on the topic. This would take me about ten minutes, I guess, and I might have to pay for the original essay if I wanted it to be any good. |
| *Using Unlikely Comparison* | |
| Write an essay comparing "Harrison Bergeron" to the story "The Lottery." | Done. Took me about a minute. Do you want that double-spaced? |
| Write an essay comparing "Harrison Bergeron" to W. H. Auden's poem "The Unknown Citizen." | This one's a little trickier than the other comparison one, but it just takes a little CTRL-C and a couple of sentences of my own. I don't even really have to change the conclusion of the essay I found except to add in the right titles. *(Note: CTRL-C is student shortcut for cutting and pasting electronically.)* |
| *Using Creativity and Personal Experience* | |
| Imagine you could spend one day in the world of "Harrison Bergeron" and talk to the characters in the story. Write a letter to the U.S. Handicapper General describing your experiences and your views on the society within the story after your visit. | The personal voice makes this one harder, but not too hard. I could probably do it mainly by changing pronouns with the find and replace function in Word and with a bit of formatting. Most teachers wouldn't catch on. |
| *Using a Quotation as a Starting Place* | |
| "The year was 2091, and everyone was finally equal." Write an essay in which you evaluate the truth of this statement within the story. | How long do you want it to be? I can give you one page, three pages, or five pages right now. I just Googled the line and the essays came up first. |

*Figure 6.1*

OK, this experiment is set-up; of course a few bright students can find a way to cheat if they're really trying. Still, the answer to the problem of plagiarism is not so simple, I believe, as tweaking prompts. That might help, and it might even be good practice in general—I wouldn't want to send freshmen off with instructions simply to "write an essay about this work" under any circumstances. But we have to go deeper, reconsidering not just how we word our prompts but also how we deliver writing and reading instruction itself.

Not every pundit, I should mention, reacts to plagiarism simply by encouraging teachers to make tougher or more obscure assignments. Professor Greg Van Belle (2001), for instance, in an online article titled "How Cheating Helps Drive Better Instruction," suggests some positive reforms that might arise from the prevalence of plagiarized work, including the suggestion to rotate the curriculum and to focus on the process assignments demand rather than merely the product. In a similar article called "Four Reasons to Be Happy About Internet Plagiarism," Russell Hunt (2007) speculates on the benefits of reconsidering traditional assignment models, grading practices, and ways of disseminating knowledge.

These writers may compose their titles with shock value in mind, but perhaps a bit of shock is merited here. Our goal, after all, is not merely to refocus our time from catching plagiarism to *foiling* the plagiarists, it's to *prevent* plagiarism from being necessary or desirable in the first place. Yet in many articles on the subject, prevention is, at the least, underaddressed; I scoured numerous major news sources for information about the Christine Pelton case, yet not one of them questioned the curricular goals or instructional process of the sophomore leaf project on which the students purportedly cheated. Pelton may well have been a model teacher and have instilled in her students a deep sense of ownership and purpose, making the transgressions that much more egregious, but I'll never know from the stories on the subject. It's not so much that the leaf project may or may not have been a sound instructional project as that no one thought it important to ask; even those willing to address the reasons students cheat often place more emphasis on the misguided understanding *students* have of sound writing process than on any substantial reforms *teachers* might make to their classes. Alfie Kohn (2007) notes a similar attitude toward the subject in his article "Who's Cheating Whom?" He describes a 2006 *New York Times* article on professors' reactions to widespread cheating:

> In every example cited in the article, the students were figuring out ways to consult their notes during exams; in one case, a student was caught using a computer spell-check program. . . . Even here, the intent appeared to be foiling cheaters rather than improving the quality of

assessment and instruction. Or, to put it differently, the goal was to find ways to prevent students from being *able* to cheat rather than addressing the reasons they *wanted* to cheat—or what the instructors *regarded* as cheating (and why).

In the sections that follow, I hope to equip teachers with tools to do more than merely reword their prompts, though that may be a first step toward redesigning assignments and reforming the learning process of students.

## Prompt Attention: Assigning Analytical and Personal Essays

A colleague of mine, Jonas Holdeman, often compares the learning he tries to elicit from students to the education of a golfer. Never mind that most of his students, like me, couldn't tell a five iron from a hockey stick; the metaphor ultimately makes sense to them. The golfer, Jonas says, has all sorts of training aids and gadgets available to him. There exist, according to numerous websites on the topic, items like the hinged trainer, the weighted club, and the slice corrector. There are books and websites, private instructors, videos, golf simulators.

No matter what tools you use, Jonas tells his classes, the real lesson comes sooner or later—you walk out onto the course and take a swing. All by yourself. You either whack the ball in a straight line or you don't.

In the field of writing and writing assessment, we need to keep sight of the ultimate goal; we want students, at some point, to take the swing on their own. An essay prompt is our version of a weighted club. It's an aid to get students thinking, to point them in the right direction. It's a means, not the end—I want students to leave my classroom, eventually, with the ability to formulate prompts for themselves, to determine the topics that need attention and to write about those topics fluidly and with skill. I want them to be able to adjust their swings, as it were, to the needs of the course and the changing terrain; to do that as writers, they'll need ingrained skills, not just good grades.

To teach writing skills, then, we need to do more than assign a prompt, have students write, and tell them what they've done wrong. We need to design instructional strategies that help students write well in

> ### Voices from the Classroom
>
> My prompts don't really lend themselves to plagiarism. It's tough to pass off what someone else says when I ask you to write something personal and you're in the ninth grade. You probably wouldn't have all those really grandiose ideas, anyway. Those prompts make it easier for me, but I still talk about it—I still tell them, "Don't even try to get something past me," and I show them how I catch them.
>
> —*Ninth-grade teacher*

the first place, encourage them to revise written work, and most of all, make writing a rewarding experience that's more than just a chore one completes for a grade. We also need to encourage the higher-order thinking that will allow students to produce meaningful writing *without* a prompt when the time for it comes.

The suggestions that follow cover three areas of essay assignment—topic development, writing process, and revision—and discuss how tuning each might help stem plagiarism in the classroom.

### Subjects and Objectives: Developing Topics and Prompts

Earlier in this chapter I discussed the common wisdoms shared by many writers about plagiarism proofing: narrow the focus of assignments, use unlikely comparisons, make writing assignments creative. I mentioned that these suggestions irk me somewhat; for instance, I want students to write, sometimes, formal and academic analyses. But when I think about both personal and analytical writing, no suggestion bothers me more than making my prompts more specific. I do understand the value of this approach, particularly in lower grades when students are learning to construct, say, an introductory paragraph for the first time. But the advice is often given for *college* teachers, who I'd hope are concerned with the sophisticated investigation of texts. The problem? The more the teacher narrows an assignment, the less a student is asked to think about the object of discussion, whether it's the work of Carl Sandburg or Carl Sagan. Specificity may sometimes avert plagiarism, but it also averts ownership of topics, creativity in approach, and higher-order cognition.

Here's an example: Imagine I assign the students in my AP comparative government class an essay on ethnicity in Nigeria. That's already a fairly esoteric subject for an American student, but there's plenty of material from which to plagiarize. So let's say I narrow the topic (and run a quick web search to be sure there are no easily accessible papers out there already, or if there are, to be sure that I'll recognize them); I ask for papers, with sources, explaining the need for the clause in the Nigerian constitution that requires a presidential candidate to receive 25 percent of the vote in two-thirds of the states in order to win. A model response will explain that requiring such a distribution of voters ensures that a candidate garners support from more than one geographically oriented ethnic group and will investigate the tensions between the major ethnicities that require such a law; at the same time, however, that topic all but guarantees that students will *not* consider, for instance, the role of religion in ethnic disputes, issues of cultural identity or gender, the history of British colonization and its effect on ethnicity, or a host of other semipolitical issues that might provide interesting thinking about ethnicity in the region. By specifying a narrow area of discussion, I rule out broader understanding.

Now let's investigate another model. Take a topic that's more easily plagiarized—an essay on a novel about Nigeria, *Things Fall Apart*. Should I simply ask students to write an essay about the novel, they can pop online and print one out. But that's not the point, because if that's the assignment I make, I haven't really taught much of anything about the process of thinking deeply about a work of literature. If, on the other hand, I ask students to write a personal reflection stemming from the novel, perhaps a discussion of the role of a father in family decisions, I may encourage deep thinking at the expense of academic investigation (which is fine sometimes, but not on every occasion).

When I make essay assignments, I commit myself first of all to the idea that process matters and that to demonstrate the process I'll have to use some class time. I *could* use that class time to have students write an actual essay, but that doesn't seem the most profitable allocation of time to me. Involving students in a step-by-step discussion, on the other hand, is a part of the writing process that can't readily be replicated outside of class. Here's a process I use:

I begin by putting students into small groups of four or five and asking them to brainstorm. "With your group," I say, "come up with a list of possible essay topics to explore. Anything reasonable goes, here, and we're not worried yet about thesis statements, just general areas you might investigate. Be creative. If it helps, divide a sheet of paper into columns labeled 'Theme,' 'Character,' 'Setting,' 'Symbol,' and 'Style.'" Because I've already modeled this exercise with the whole class, students take to this sort of brainstorming readily, and here's the thing: The book's not out of bounds. Neither is the Internet. Neither is collaborative discussion; anything that might conceivably be called plagiarism is, at this point, merely part of the process. In order to include everyone, I might have groups assign roles (I learned this trick from Harvey Daniels' book, *Literature Circles* [2001]); in this case, I might have a recorder, a group moderator, a presenter, and a researcher. I could also suggest assigning one area of the novel, such as symbols, to each person in the group, then combining and discussing.

When the groups are finished with their individual investigation, we collaborate more: we list *all* of the potential topics on the board and discuss them as a class. As we go, we pick out the nuances raised by different phrasings and approaches; one group, for instance, has suggested Achebe's inclusion of animals as a motif while another has suggested that the characters' *perceptions* of animals reveal important attitudes of the society. We mention possible evidence, as well—scenes from the novel that could be used as proof.

The next task is for each student to develop a *topic* into a *thesis*. What is there to say about a particular area of the book? If, for example, the

Discussion questions for faculty about designing assignments and assessments are available online in the *Plagiarism Study Guide* at www.heinemann .com/gilmore.

author uses animals as symbols, what are they symbols for and why does it matter? On the second day of class, I have each student share a possible thesis, even if it isn't yet fully refined, and then put students into pairs or groups once more based on the type of thesis they've chosen to investigate—thematic, character based, symbolism driven, and so on.

In pairs or groups, the students discuss the possible thesis, look at the text to find examples or quotations that might be useful, and ask one another questions to hone the argument into a specific take on the story that will pay off by the conclusion of the paper. In a technology-rich environment, this conversation could happen electronically through email, a discussion forum, a chat room, or a wiki, and then I could have a transcript; personal interaction with note taking works just as well, however.

Individual students then develop a thesis statement and introductory paragraph. At this point, I can include more group work or individual responses from me orally or in writing, or I can have the class move on to completing a full essay. Either way, I've accomplished, I hope, multiple goals:

- the students have taken ownership of their own topics, eliminating, to some extent, the desire simply to copy someone else's work;

- topics are individually and creatively defined, making it difficult to find papers that fit just right online;

- collaborative efforts have instilled a sense of dialogue and community in the students without encouraging simple copying;

- the students have reflected on several aspects of the novel and thought deeply about at least one of those aspects; and

- the papers will be more interesting to read and score.

Personal essays and content-area writing can follow the same model of collaboration, step-by-step thesis development, and individual creation. Might a student plagiarize? Sure, she might, but the topics that come from such a process are no more or less ripe for copying than those I create myself, while the sense of investment on the part of the students is much higher—a factor that I believe makes plagiarism less likely to occur.

### Write and Wrong: Encouraging Originality During the Writing Process
No matter how much prewriting, planning, or discussion takes place, most plagiarism occurs when a student actually sits down, looks at a blank computer screen, checks the clock, and encounters that sinking realization that this assignment will *never* get done on time. Ultimately, students have to figure this out for themselves; the older they get, the

more responsible they need to be about writing on their own time. But here are a few writing process considerations that might help diminish the likelihood of plagiarism:

- *Require students to complete some writing in class.* Yes, for the most part, in-class writing is less likely to be plagiarized, but that's not the main reason to include it in your classes. No matter what grade you teach, students benefit from the practice of writing, sharing, and revising together. Note that I don't just mention writing—for writing to be a productive use of class time, I believe it must be followed by critical reading and revision. I often have students write the first paragraph of a longer piece in class, share with a peer, share any particular good sentences or questions with the class, and then complete the assignment at home. There's also, of course, a value to informal writing as a community—journal entries, fast writes, and bell ringers all have their place in any subject area—but don't forget the value of formal writing, either.

- *Have students practice metacognition.* The act of thinking about thinking—or, in this case, writing about writing—offers students the chance to reflect on strategies, planning, and the process itself. It's also difficult to complete a metacognitive assignment about a piece you've plagiarized. If students know this step is coming, they'll be less likely to skip its precursor: original composition.

- *Make assignments due in pieces.* Again, this advice might be applied differently for different age groups, but why not set due dates of a paragraph per day rather than five at the end of a week? Even in an AP English class I might try this approach once in a while to force students to slow down, to think again about paragraph and sentence composition, and just to give the class a break during a high-pressure week.

- *Encourage originality through collaboration.* The process for discovering topics I described earlier can also work during the writing process. If partners have a stake in each other's work (when they're assigned to check in with each other's progress each day, for instance, or when they're required to read each other's rough drafts or check each other's sources), they often encourage and propel each other toward deadlines. Don't rely on partnerships or groups to do your work for you, but try them out during the writing process—if they work, so much the better for the students.

- *Have students plan strategies for attributing as they write.* It's tricky to balance the creative process with the tedious logistics of attribution. Students who have a strategy in place—whether it's using note cards or just bookmarking sites—don't have to slow down the rhythm of writing. Personally, I attribute in units; I note URLs or page numbers on a desktop sticky note or in a spreadsheet as I write, then I format that piece of my bibliography when I finish writing the section.

### Take It Again: Revision and Academic Integrity

In my book *"Is It Done Yet?": Teaching Adolescents the Art of Revision*, I wrote the following:

> Revision, treated as an ally and not a necessary evil, can help get past some of the hurdles in the way of good student writing: boredom, fear, and resignation. Offering students the tools to revise content, in particular, not only improves writing but the attitude of writers. It encourages students to take pride in and care with what they write, to invest themselves in it before hacking it up in the name of syntax or grammar. (Gilmore 2007, 8)

I went back and reread those words, thinking about plagiarism. I do still believe that revision, often looked upon as the most tedious step in the process (one teacher I know defines revision as "doing it over with better handwriting"), can in fact be the step that encourages students to feel most positive about their work and thus increase their desire to write. That's because revision is the time not just for fixing errors but for carefully crafting both ideas and style into a sophisticated whole.

In thinking about revision as an antiplagiarism tool in particular, I'd offer a few thoughts that might help:

- *It's not plagiarism until you actually take credit for it.* A rough draft without proper citation format is still just a rough draft, and students might learn more from comments that require them to rewrite with proper citation than from accusations. That's not the same thing, mind you, as not reporting plagiarism, though the line between the two may be fine and may reflect the nuances of the assignment and teaching approach you use.

- *Content revision may make plagiarism impossible.* In *"Is It Done Yet?"* I spend a large chunk of the book discussing the idea that revision must start with the broadest strokes—revisiting the topic, argument, organization, and overall approach to constructing a full essay or written piece. A standard college essay (or personal statement) is a good example of this; a plagiarized piece probably isn't worth the paper it's copied on, since the whole point of a successful essay lies in its uniqueness. Any run-of-the-mill personal statement with which I help a student (carefully, mind you, since originality matters here as much as anywhere) is probably going back to the drawing board whether it's plagiarized or not; I won't be satisfied with it until it clearly reflects the interests and personality of the author and only the author. We'd hope all writing would work that way, and revisiting the content and argument of formal, academic writing can also render plagiarism in the first draft useless at times.

- *Revising style can also render plagiarism useless.* On the first essay I assign each year, I have students revise a single aspect of their writing each day for five days in a row. On day 1 we revise sentence structure only; on day 2 verbs; then adjectives; then punctuation (tied closely to syntax); and finally, turns of phrase. By the time the students are finished, most of the sentences bear no resemblance to the originals. I can't complete this process with every paper students compose, but giving students the tools to use subordination, solid vocabulary, and advanced sentence forms is a good way to ensure that they'll rarely feel that someone else said it better than they themselves ever could.

Paying attention to the *whole* process of writing, from topic formulation to revision to final draft, isn't just a good way to combat plagiarism; it's strong pedagogy. By the time you've broken down the writing process into steps and then reassembled it with your students, discussions about plagiarism may take an entirely different shape, and incidences of it will, I hope, decline or disappear altogether.

## Research Assignments

Earlier I mentioned a book I wrote on the process of revision; after finishing it, I received a draft of a publicity brochure that described the title ("Is It Done Yet?") as "4 of the most dreaded words in the English classroom." At the time, though I approved of the copywriter's clever approach to selling the book, I suspected that I could come up with four-word phrases that students

---

### Voices from the Classroom

My history teacher asks these questions, like, "How many people like cheese?" And the textbook says, "60 percent of people like cheese." How do you not plagiarize that? But then she gets mad if I copy from the book. And on her essays, it's not like you'd look it up on the Internet, but they're fact based. But then last year's history teacher allowed us to copy up to three words from the text, and my freshman teacher gave all opinion essays and diary entries that you couldn't plagiarize. It's all stuff I could copy if I want; I *try* to do it myself, but sometimes it's just impossible.

—*Darlene, age sixteen*

might fear more ("Today is test day," for instance, or "Here are your grades") and I *knew* that I could think of four-word phrases that would strike greater fear into the hearts of English teachers: "The photocopier is broken," "Your triple latte spilled," or perhaps "Today's inservice topic: calculus."

But if the phrase were limited to two words, the clear winner for terror-inducing, knee-knocking, hand-wringing combination would be "research paper." Students, teachers, and pretty much anyone who's ever gone to school will start to mew like a wounded cat when you bring the subject up. I've even met professional *researchers* who shudder at the memory of the research papers they had to write in high school; one can well imagine Archimedes giving up any thoughts about buoyancy or water displacement and just staying in the bathtub all day if he'd thought his experiments would have to be accompanied by 150 perfectly filled out note cards, a formal outline, and an annotated bibliography.

Some teachers do love the research paper, of course—the structure and order appeals to them, perhaps, or they welcome a chance to broaden an assignment through incorporating the arguments and voices of critics and experts. But by and large the traditional research paper seems to be slipping away from language arts classrooms. In my survey of eighty high school students from across the state of Tennessee, I asked the students about research papers in their schools. Here are a few of the striking results of the students' responses:

- 65 percent of the students had completed a research paper or project in their English classes during the previous year, while only 38 percent had written a research paper for a social studies class.

- Of those who wrote a research paper for an English class, 67 percent focused on a historical event or current events issue, not on a particular text or group of texts (I include in this grouping papers on the life of an author without an analysis of that author's writing).

- The average number of pages for research papers in English was 8.5, for social studies, 3.5.

These results were, to me, unsurprising but telling. To begin with, one might wish to believe that the one-third of students *not* conducting research for English classes are the same one-third who *are* researching for social studies classes, but that would probably involve a fair bit of self-deception. So a good third of teachers have given up on research entirely. The salient question: *Why* are these teachers relinquishing the research

### Voices from the Classroom

To some extent, the idea of, say, looking up how a volcano works is almost asinine, because you can do it in thirty seconds. The nature of our middle school assignments has changed to analysis, interpretation, and compare and contrast, because just researching and regurgitating facts isn't a challenge anymore, if it ever was. That curbs plagiarism, but the point is the analysis, how to relate information to what you're learning in class.

—*Seventh-grade teacher*

paper? Is it because they don't value it as a source of learning, because they don't want to grade lengthy projects, because it takes up too much class time, because they don't believe their students will do a good job with the assignment, because of plagiarism concerns?

I suspect that many of these reasons apply for some teachers, but more than anything else I suspect that many teachers—even those who still doggedly dredge up the research paper assignment year after year—remain mired in a fairly narrow idea of what research entails and how it manifests in student writing. Consider: in my survey, two-thirds of those writing research papers for English classes (more than the total number who completed papers at all for social studies classes) chose to write about—or were assigned—topics that had nothing to do with literary analysis. The most common topic mentioned in student responses was writing about "the biography of an author," but other students noted topics such as the Bay of Pigs, immigration to the United States, genocide in Africa, China's family planning policy, and shootings in school communities. It was rare enough for a student to mention actual texts in conjunction with writing about a writer's life, but almost none mentioned topics that actually focused on an analysis of a text's rhetorical or thematic material.

But let's be optimistic about this. Students might be

- writing issues-based and history-based research papers that will be graded by both English and social studies teachers;

- writing papers on issues related to the content of literature they're reading;

- studying the style and rhetoric of nonfiction primary documents as they conduct research; or

- using research on an author's life to springboard into a deeper understanding of the themes and rhetoric of that author's writing.

Do you believe any of these possibilities?

I'm certain there exist occasional collaborations between English and social studies teachers (or between teachers in other disciplines—science and history, or art and language arts), and surely our best students intuit lessons about texts from the independent study of an author's life, but across the board the majority of language arts teachers, I imagine, assign the same kind of research papers they encountered in their own high school classes. Many English teachers I talk to see the research paper as a necessary evil that imparts to students the value of methodical and systematic research; in other words, the topic isn't important, but the process is.

In part, I agree with the value of teaching the research process. There's nothing inherently *bad* about the note cards and outlines, unless it's that they tend to turn students off to research entirely, but so do most difficult and potentially tedious assignments (think vocabulary and grammar exercises) unless they're presented in a way that makes them exciting, potentially useful to students, or both. Although it's been years since I used note cards for my own research, I constantly double-check my own notes to be sure I've included all of the information that might have gone on a note card when I wrote papers as a student.

So my issue is not with carefully teaching the process. It's with the idea that the content is irrelevant to learning that process. Set aside for a moment the obvious argument that a randomly chosen or assigned topic isn't as likely to spur student engagement as one that is self-selected; there's a deeper issue here. I maintain the following:

- There's a value in teaching students to write about many subjects, not just literature, but such papers should ideally be developed through writing across the curriculum and cross-curricular teaching.

- It is possible for students to engage in productive and meaningful research directly related to the disciplines of language arts and literary studies—or whatever subject is the focus of the assignment.

- Research papers that analyze texts actually encourage deeper and more thoughtful research than those that merely report on a biography.

- The current trend in language arts classes toward assigning personally relevant, informal research topics to raise interest and discourage plagiarism reflects good teaching practice, but we shouldn't limit students by never asking them to work on a formal research paper of any sort.

In other words, what we have here is a discipline problem. No, not the kind that you encountered on your first day as a new teacher when you felt sure that the students could smell fear and would lock you in your own supply closet before the end of the day. I'm talking about the disciplines we *teach*—English, history, science, geography. Why are students in literature classes writing papers better suited to a history classroom when an American history class may not require a research paper at all? Why are students writing only about the lives of authors when we could be furthering their critical thinking skills about the works those authors produce?

Our first question, then, is this: What's the point of the research paper at all? What are we trying to accomplish, and for whom? And addressing the purpose of the assignment will lead us, in turn, to what students will write *about* and how we structure assignments.

### Getting to the Point: The Role of Purpose, Audience, and Topic in Assigning the Research Paper

What do we hope to accomplish when we assign a research paper? I posed this question to several of my colleagues and received, in various wordings, responses that indicate the need for students to learn

- knowledge about a particular subject or academic area
- information-retrieval skills
- the conventions and format of research-based writing
- what professional models of research and source analysis entail
- the challenges and benefits of structuring and writing an extensive composition
- how to integrate the ideas of others and their own ideas into a coherent, sustained argument

Some teachers responded to my query with other thoughts, as well: "I don't know why I'm teaching the research paper in eighth grade," one said, "instead of the history or science teacher assigning it. But I am." Another responded, "The research paper is a part of our benchmarks and standards, and it takes three weeks to get through—about the length of time I could spend on one novel or preparing students to perform a play. I'm never certain whether that's good or bad—am I happy to have three weeks of cut-and-dried class work for students to complete, or should I despair over teaching less literature, demanding as that is on my planning schedule?" For these teachers, reflection on the purpose and goals of the assignment isn't a luxury, it's a necessity.

The six responses to my question listed previously are worthy objectives; students need to learn these skills. Yet they're fairly disparate in nature. The first, gaining knowledge, isn't in fact a skill at all and might be as well accomplished through other means. And then take, for instance, the objective of teaching students information-retrieval skills. Should students be capable of finding sources in a library? Sure they should; they should also be able to look up Spanish words they don't know in a dictio-

**YOU NEED TO KNOW: Other Results of My Survey**

My survey of Tennessee students revealed a few other interesting student perceptions. Here are two worth considering:

1. Students listed as the most effective ways of learning about specific topics, in order, discussion, lectures (but only by dynamic and interesting teachers), narratives and fiction, primary documents, readings from textbooks, and research projects involving writing. That list suggests volumes to me about the antipathy students feel toward the traditional research project but doesn't dissuade me from feeling that research is a necessary skill for students to possess.

2. When asked how often their teachers actively discussed the differences in expectations for research papers by discipline (i.e., the difference between what an English teacher might expect from such a paper and what a science teacher might expect), 25 percent of students responded that teachers held such discussions often, 40 percent sometimes, and 35 percent rarely or never. In follow-up discussions, it became clear to me that such differences in expectations were a major source of frustration to many students.

nary or use the advanced functions of a calculator when necessary to figure out a difficult math problem. Those skills are useful, but they're not the equivalent of language fluency or the ability to construct a bridge. Similarly, we must hold in perspective the skills we ask of our students as researchers—those that are building blocks and those that involve the construction of entire structures.

## *Teaching Opportunities*

Research papers and projects should not be used as a means to an end. If they are, they'll turn into exactly the sort of tiresome chore that allows students to rationalize acts of academic dishonesty. Here, then, are recommendations for making research papers an integral part of your syllabus rather than an addendum to it:

- *Make research topics discipline specific and connect them to other work in the course.* A student who is assigned to write five pages on the life cycle of the sponge just because that's the only topic left on a list is more likely to plagiarize than one writing about a high-interest topic that's been discussed and seems vital to the curriculum.

- *Assess research papers for content as much as for procedure, if not more.* Overwhelmingly, the students I surveyed in 2007 reported that research writing completed in language arts classes was graded, first and foremost, for style, organization, argument, grammar, mechanics. Social studies teachers, on the other hand, reportedly graded *only* on the basis of content and historical accuracy, rarely marking style or language at all. Few of the projects required revision of any sort (too many teachers, I suspect, didn't want to read the papers a second time, and I don't blame them; once you've read about the life cycle of a sponge, you've probably pretty much gotten all you want from the paper). I suggest, I hope without being too critical of busy classroom teachers, that such approaches undervalue student words and the effort they put into them and thus make it easier for students to fall back on shortcuts. If you want good writing, it needs to be taken seriously as academic work (and therefore needs to have an interesting focus in the first place).

- *Specify an audience.* Most teachers I know who suggest that a specific audience can help deter plagiarism mean by this that students who write first-person, personal accounts or complete oral histories are less likely to copy their work, and they're right. But there are numerous other audiences for research work, and the critical review, mock journal article, political briefing, and presentation all have their place. Discussing audience is important; providing one is even better. One science teacher in our school has students report their findings on environmental policy directly to local politicians each year; the assignment encourages students to check and double-check sources and points. A similar effect might be gained from making parents, administrators, other students, or the audience of the World Wide Web into readers of student writing.

- *Consider products other than writing in conjunction with writing.* I'm not a huge fan of removing writing from the research process altogether, though I do have students complete other projects in addition to longer research papers. I also like to ask students to write part of a project and use another medium for presentation: PowerPoint, Photo Story, video documentary, recorded interviews, website FAQ pages, group presentations, dramatic reenactments, and visual art of various sorts all make projects more interesting overall and, even in conjunction with written pieces, reduce the likelihood of plagiarism.

With enough attention and with careful planning, the term paper doesn't have to seem just plain terminal. I believe the value of teaching students to research—and to include research in their writing—overweighs the simple desire to avoid plagiarism, but that doesn't mean plagiarism won't be an issue if students feel disengaged. Assignment planning is as important with research papers as with any academic activity, but the results can be worth it.

## Making the Grade: Adjusting Rubrics

One of the funnier moments I've witnessed in class came about when a student took one of the six-point rubrics I was showing the class, cut it and taped it into a cube, and threw it at me. "Duck!" he yelled. "It's a rubric's cube!"

Much has been written recently about the perceived dangers of rubrics. Maja Wilson's radical take on the value of rubrics in her 2006 book *Rethinking Rubrics in Writing Assessment*, for example, is convincing— she argues, in part, that rubrics stifle creativity rather than assessing it— but I still feel rubrics have value. At the same time, I'd argue that good practice requires us to reconsider, as Wilson suggests, the ways in which we use rubrics and assessments of many sorts (I discuss grades specifically in the next chapter, so here I'll focus on the actual form of assessments), and that rethinking in this way can also help us combat plagiarism. Here are some of the suggestions I make to teachers about assessment in general and rubrics in particular:

- *Do not let rubrics take the place of written or oral commentary on writing.* Reducing a student's writing to a number and a box of prepackaged comments may increase your speed as a grader and may feel more objective, but it reduces the authenticity of your response instead of increasing it. Rubrics that include commentary, however, can focus teacher comments in a way that allows students to put those comments into a broader context of expectations and personal improvement, thus increasing students' motivation to write original work, as well.

- *Involve students in the design of rubrics, grading scales, and scoring criteria.* I can't stress the value of this step enough—though it takes time, nothing leads to more authentic assessment (and thus more student interest in meeting expectations) than for students to set the expectations themselves. Completed as a class, a scoring rubric can be a valuable teaching tool in and of itself; it also becomes an effective springboard for class discussions about writing.

- *Rubrics and scoring criteria should reward risk taking, original thinking, and creativity.* The worst rubrics hem students in, quite often in the name of valuing process over product. Process is important, but following directions shouldn't take precedence over creativity in every instance. A writing rubric can easily include risk taking among the criteria for high-scoring papers right beside style and mechanics—of course, risk taking that pays off is even more valuable, and risk taking for its own sake is not always desirable. That difference, too, can provide rich ground for discussion with students.

The creation of the rubric's cube may have been a joke, but I didn't miss an underlying metaphor: to students, a rubric can sometimes seem as false and random as the roll of a die. To make assessment work in favor of academic honesty, we must instill it with a genuine interest in student learning, not in getting through the stack of papers more quickly (though believe me, I know as well as anyone the desire to decrease the size of the stack). From assignment to assessment, that genuine focus on learning is the surest way to keep students not just from plagiarizing but from even *thinking* about it.

## Works Cited

Daniels, Harvey. 2001. *Literature Circles: Voice and Choice in Book Clubs and Reading Groups.* Portland, ME: Stenhouse.

Gilmore, Barry. 2007. *"Is It Done Yet?": Teaching Adolescents the Art of Revision.* Portsmouth, NH: Heinemann.

Hunt, Russell. 2007. "Four Reasons to Be Happy About Internet Plagiarism." St. Thomas University. www.stu.ca/~hunt/4reasons.htm (accessed Mar. 23, 2008).

Kohn, Alfie. 2007. "Who's Cheating Whom?" *Phi Delta Kappan.* www.alfiekohn.org/teaching/cheating.htm (accessed Mar. 23, 2008).

Van Belle, Greg. 2001. "How Cheating Helps Drive Better Instruction." *Plagiarized.com.* www.plagiarized.com/vanb.html (accessed Mar. 23, 2008).

Wilson, Maja. 2006. *Rethinking Rubrics in Writing Assessment.* Portsmouth, NH: Heinemann.

# 7 *The Big Picture*

## *The Role of School Culture*

As I worked on this book, I received numerous emails from friends pointing out plagiarism in the news: I was working on Chapter 3 when Barack Obama was accused of plagiarizing material from other political speeches and I was halfway through Chapter 5 when a presidential aide resigned amid a plagiarism scandal. A major network reported that "recent [cheating] scandals have rocked . . . the highest-performing schools in the nation, where the pressure to get into an Ivy League college is intense and parents buy into the academic game" (James 2008). By the time you read these words, more recent public cases will surely spring to mind. If you believe the news, there's no one—not even among prominent historians, journalists, politicians, or authors—who's beyond the crime (or error) of usurping others' words and ideas.

The cases reported in the news don't *always* lead to severe consequences, but most of the time they do. Why, then, do others not get the message? Why is it hard to make students see the dangers of academic dishonesty? Why does the ethics gap between student perceptions of right and wrong and school policy continue to exist?

To answer those questions, I suggest we examine plagiarism in a context broader than the individual classroom or student. Individual school culture and the culture of schools as a whole may play a bigger role in creating perceptions than written policies or isolated experiences. Consider, for instance, a study conducted by professors at the Rochester Institute of Technology in 2002, as summarized in an article titled "Students Plagiarize Less than Many Think, a New Study Finds":

> While 24.5 percent of students reported "often," "very frequently," or "sometimes" having cut and pasted text from the Internet without proper citation, 27.6 percent reported having done the same with conventional texts. Meanwhile, more than 90 percent of students reported that their peers "often," "very frequently," or "sometimes" copied text without citation from conventional sources. (Kellogg 2002)

## TOP TEN: Values of Ethical Schools

The following list comes from an article titled "Individual and Contextual Influences on Academic Dishonesty: A Multicampus Investigation" (McCabe and Trevino 1997). It describes, as one researcher notes, "the activities that support higher levels of student integrity" (Nagelson 2007, 3). Such policies and activities include

1. realizing and affirming academic integrity as an institutional core value
2. promoting a commitment to lifelong learning
3. establishing the role of teachers as both guides and mentors
4. assisting students in understanding how the Internet can help and also hurt them
5. encouraging students to take responsibility for academic integrity
6. providing assurance that students know and understand expectations
7. creating and using fair forms of assessment
8. decreasing the opportunities students have to be academically dishonest
9. dealing with academic dishonesty when it happens
10. assisting with defining and supporting campuswide academic standards for behavior

Consider these figures through analogy: What if a survey revealed that one-quarter of students claim not to get enough sleep each night but that nine out of ten believe their peers don't get enough sleep? Which result would you tend to believe? With plagiarism, it's easier to think that students might lie about the frequency with which they themselves retreat to acts of dishonesty, but the staggering differences in the figures make it difficult to ignore the idea that students' *perceptions* of their academic culture is not the same as the reality. Students think cheating goes on all the time, whether it does or not.

Culture matters, and culture is not created by a single teacher or administrator, though it's worth remembering that classrooms do have distinct cultures as well as schools. Research backs up the idea, however, that a culture of integrity forms not just at the classroom level but also at an

## YOU NEED TO KNOW: Talking It Out

How much difference does it make when teachers discuss honor codes, academic integrity, and cheating in their classrooms? Take a look at the following paragraph from the *Council Chronicle*, published by the National Council of Teachers of English:

> Anne Ruggles Gere, director of NCTE's Squire Office for Policy Research, reports, "Among students in grades 3–5, when the teacher did discuss online cheating, 61 percent of students felt copying information from the Internet was cheating. That number dropped to 49.1 percent when teachers did not discuss cheating. Similarly, 22.6 percent of students in grades 6–12 felt copying from the Internet was okay when teachers discussed the issue, but that number jumped to 36.9 percent among students whose teachers did not discuss the issue. At both levels the differences were statistically significant." (2005)

institutional level. As one investigation put it, "an institution's ability to develop a shared understanding and acceptance of its academic integrity policies has a significant and substantive impact on student perceptions of their peers' behavior" (McCabe, Trevino, and Butterfield 2001, 222).

Several aspects of school culture relate directly to the presence or absence of plagiarism: competition, rewards, honor codes, faculty modeling, and student activities. A note of caution here: It's tempting for teachers to feel that control of some of these aspects of education lies beyond the influence of the individual educator. Yet school culture is built both through overarching policies and messages and also classroom by classroom; students' most direct contact is with teachers, so teachers help shape perception. Not only can schools change the educational environment in which students operate, but teachers can change the climate of schools.

## Unhealthy Competition? How Grades and Rankings Encourage Dishonesty

"Tell me why you got an A on that writing assignment," I say to one of my better students; call her Melanie.

"I did everything the teacher asked," Melanie answers. "I used the right number of sources, I wrote it long enough, and I didn't make any mistakes."

"That's how," I say. "Does that answer why?"

Melanie considers this for a moment. "Well, it tells me why the teacher gave me an A, I guess. She wanted me to learn to do it right."

"What about content? Did she grade you on the quality of your ideas?"

"Yeah, I think so," she says.

"How do you know?"

Melanie shows me the essay. "She wrote, 'good thinking and originality,' at the top. Then she just marked the rubric that says I did everything right."

"OK, so why did you do everything right?"

"To get an A."

"What about good thinking and originality?" I ask.

Melanie frowns. "Well, I think I did OK, but really I just answered the question. I know what's on the rubric, though, and I know that I have to do the sources and all that to get a top grade. That's what I care about most."

"How come?" I ask.

"College. And my parents. And I just feel good when I get an A."

"Would you ever cheat to get an A?"

"No," Melanie answers. "But I know a whole lot of people who would."

There are critics who charge that grading and ranking of any type are the main enemies of real education, and while I can't say I wholly disagree with them, I also understand the practicalities faced by classroom teachers who must operate within the conventional system of As and Fs. Out of interest, though, consider the voices of those who dislike conventional grading systems. Maja Wilson, author of *Rethinking Rubrics in Writing Assessment*, whom I mentioned in the last chapter, suggests that written commentaries as opposed to grades (determined by rubrics) "require teachers to foster insight into the writing process and provide opportunities for students to engage in it—they require us to *teach writing* rather than simply to assign, correct, and return essays" (2006, 86). She goes on to suggest that "as long as grades or other forms of ranking are the

> ### Voices from the Classroom
>
> Long ago, I realized that I care more about receiving good grades than actually learning. Even though I realize this is wrong, that knowledge should be more important than report cards, I cannot seem to change my attitude. As a straight A student who aims one day to be valedictorian, I want good grades whether I deserve them or not.
>
> Quite frankly, I do blame the system. The competitiveness, the honoring of principal's list students, the prestige—it all just encourages students to get good grades by any means necessary. Everything is a grade, and grades are all people see.
>
> —*Ainsley, age sixteen*

ultimate goal of writing assessment, we will not truly be able to claim assessment for teaching and learning" (87). A similar opinion comes, again, from Alfie Kohn, who related his experience in an article titled "The Trouble with Rubrics":

> I'd been looking for an alternative to grades because research shows three reliable effects when students are graded: They tend to think less deeply, avoid taking risks, and lose interest in the learning itself. The ultimate goal of authentic assessment must be the elimination of grades. But rubrics actually help to *legitimate* grades by offering a new way to derive them. They do nothing to address the terrible reality of students who have been led to focus on getting As rather than on making sense of ideas. (2006, 12)

A group of thoughtful teachers could argue all day long about the value or lack of value inherent in grading systems. To some extent, however, I'd expect any thoughtful teacher to see the point: students who focus on grades don't focus, at least as fully, on learning. And, by extension, a student who is not focused on learning is more susceptible to the temptation to plagiarize. Research conducted by psychologist Eric M. Anderman found that students who cheat tend to

- worry about school
- perceive their school as focused on grades and ability
- believe they can obtain some kind of reward for doing well in class
- attribute failure in school to outside circumstances
- avoid using deep-level cognitive processing strategies, such as trying different ways to solve a problem (APA 1998)

What's more, the temptation to cheat may be further reinforced by the common perception of students that middle and high school and college experiences with dishonesty differ:

> Most students come to college expecting it will be different from high school. Many seem to view the primary goal of high school as gaining admission to the college of their choice, and they find their academic work somewhat irrelevant, more of an obstacle to college admission than a true learning experience. Although their view may eventually change, they arrive at college thinking this is where true learning occurs. (McCabe, Trevino, and Butterfield 2001, 230)

Melanie's not a lost cause, but neither is she fully convinced about her own learning. Grades are important to her, learning is a desirable but casual by-product of achieving those grades, and she's comfortable operating in a system that is built to allow her to achieve those grades with hard work. That last point is the sticking place, however, because of the many students who aren't entirely comfortable in such a system for a variety of reasons. For these students, the alternative of cheating may seem an easier road than that of accepting lower marks in what, for them, is an arbitrary and unnecessary arrangement to begin with.

> ## Voices from the Classroom
>
> Supposedly, high school is about learning. However, since no kid actually had the choice to go of his own free will, many do not feel that academic integrity matters. No college-bound student will deny, though, that grades matter a lot. The majority of the time kids work for the grade not the knowledge. How often does one hear, "Yes, I memorized the preamble to the Declaration!" rather than "Yes, I got an A!"
>
> Personally, I care more about the grade than the knowledge. Much of the stuff I supposedly learn has little practical value, whereas grades are my future.
>
> —*Ryan, age fifteen*

What do we do, though, as teachers who must assign grades and hold students accountable for *not* completing work? I've worked in systems where I was required to assign two grades each week and in others where I was free to give students just two grades in a marking period—one for writing and one for participation, both arrived at holistically. Any experienced teacher will quickly see the particular restrictions on classroom creativity in the former system and the potential for abuse and miscommunication in the latter. Where, then, do we strike a balance?

### Teaching Opportunities

Here are some suggestions for rethinking the emphasis grading scales may unwittingly place on product over process:

- *Reward risk taking.* Build risk taking and cognitive strategies into rubrics or recognize them in comments. Consider, for instance, a student who is asked to discuss whether or not Brutus is a tragic hero in Shakespeare's *Julius Caesar*, a topic I've actually seen assigned to a sophomore English class. What happens to the student who wants to argue that Caesar is the tragic hero of the play in the early acts and Brutus the tragic hero only in the later acts? Is that student encouraged and praised or penalized for failing to answer the question? Answering the question may be important in some cases (such as standardized and state tests), and it's worth discussing such scenarios with students, but at some point creative thinking should be rewarded, as well.

- *Encourage revision.* "Students may still plagiarize when they revise at home," one teacher told me, "but most of the time, once they start an original piece, they'll want to finish it themselves." Try giving students a chance to begin their work in class, then finish through multiple revisions at home. Give credit for the revisions or build the revision process into your rubric as a step worthy of being graded in and of itself.

- *Focus on narrative and oral response to student writing.* Rather than relying on rubrics and numbered grades that categorize and rank writing, consider, on occasion at least, responding simply by writing a narrative, recording one (I use a laptop and email to deliver recorded comments), or just talking to a student about a draft or final paper. Besides lowering the pressure that might lead to plagiarism, these methods of response offer highly authentic feedback to students, allow teachers to model writing and thinking about writing, and form a personal connection between teacher and student. Recording my responses, in addition, actually takes me *less* time than writing comments on an essay.

- *Rethink honor rolls.* Yes, honor rolls reward hard workers, and I'm not calling for outright abolition of such recognition. But I've also known teachers who post the names of students who make *A*s on tests on bulletin boards, and such practice concerns me. For one thing, the same student names are likely to appear again and again, and for another, that sort of list fails to recognize the hard work of students who make *C*s but have learned a great deal in the process. The pressure created by such systems is one more influence on student decisions about integrity in school work and is worth a second look.

The point of all of these suggestions is to recognize learning whenever it occurs, whether or not that learning is reflected by high scores. Many teachers do this on a daily basis just by interacting with students, but formalizing that recognition is not a bad way to reinforce your ideas about what's important and valuable in a school setting.

> ### Voices from the Classroom
>
> The idea of having an all-knowing database of papers and words; it's almost invasive. It's much more effective to have just you and yourself and your conscience deciding what to do. The honor code provides a standard which we *should* all go by. If you don't abide by it, you eventually get screwed—later in life, just lacking the knowledge. Or getting caught and they bring up the violation of the honor code as a step toward getting kicked out of school—it's not worth it. In the short term, you get a personal gain from plagiarizing, but if you take the time to do it yourself, that's a long-term effect. But in a way and in theory the honor code discourages plagiarism; in reality, I don't think it does.
>
> —*Antonio, age fourteen*

## Making the Payoffs: Extrinsic and Intrinsic Rewards

In the traits of students who cheat that I mentioned earlier, one item bears special mention; Anderman's research found that students who cheat "believe they can obtain some kind of reward for doing well in class" (APA 1998). The article summarizing the report's findings goes on to discuss this area of student perception:

> When students believe they will receive an extrinsic benefit for doing well in class, such as getting out of homework or other assignments, they will be more likely to cheat. Dr. Anderman, lead author of the study, notes that "it is ironic that many students view the reward for doing well in the classroom as being able to get out of additional learning activities." The researchers point out that if the value of the reward is more important to the student than the academic task itself, the student may consider cheating acceptable.

In a busy learning environment—an eighth- or eleventh-grade classroom, for instance—it may be easy to make deals with students: "Do well on this test and I'll let you out of tonight's homework" or "If everyone completes this essay, we'll have cookies in class on Friday" or even "All students who make the honor roll get an extra hour of recess or lunch."

Should students earn rewards for hard work? In one sense, sure. Hard work merits recognition and praise (but don't confuse grades with evidence of hard work—they're not necessarily synonymous). Hard work also merits graduation to levels that inspire more challenge, and ideally it should lead to an intrinsic reward: the satisfaction of learning. Some may argue that it's expecting a great deal to think that a seventh grader will be grateful for the abstract reward of skill acquisition, and I concede that many adolescents would find a pizza party a bit more gratifying. At the same time, however, consider the message of the pizza party: *make good grades and get a special reward.* From there it's not a leap for a thirteen year-old to *make good grades in any way you can to get the special reward.*

> ### Voices from the Classroom
>
> The voices are better when I just give them all or nothing as a grade. They turn in the paper, they get full credit, or they don't and they get nothing. On written work, it takes the edge off—their ninth-grade voices are stunning and developing and are better because they're not worried about me circling the jots and tittles and I'm just reading for content and telling them what I think.
>
> —*Ninth-grade teacher*

### Teaching Opportunities

If you want to reinforce the rewards of learning for learning's sake, I encourage you to have students reflect on their own learning through

| What I Know—Sonnet Unit | | |
|---|---|---|
| **What I've Read** | **What I've Learned** | **What I've Written** |
| Shakespeare's sonnets | • sonnet form<br>• how to figure out a rhyme scheme<br>• extended metaphor<br>• Shakespeare's life and times<br>• new vocabulary ("erst!") | |
| | • how to divide using quatrains and a couplet<br>• how to paraphrase poems<br>• citation | Sonnet paraphrase |
| | • that I'm cynical about love<br>• how to use enjambment<br>• a bunch of good rhymes for "I got dumped after prom" | My own sonnet! |

*Figure 7.1*

metacognitive exercises. In both the short and long terms, written or oral or even artistic reflection on learning can help students recognize the inherent benefits of learning. Consider, for instance, a "What I Know" chart (my students call this a WIK). Figure 7.1 shows an example from a tenth-grade English class.

The WIK chart can be used after a single class, a unit, or even a semester or a year. Such reflection, which can also be accomplished through journaling, online discussion, oral discussion, or other informal means, is a fantastic way to have students show themselves not only how much ground they've covered but, often, why it matters to them that they've done so.

## May I Have the Honor? The Value of Honor Codes

The good news is this: honor codes work.

But watch out. The implementation of an honor code won't *eliminate* academic dishonesty, even if, statistically speaking, it reduces the frequency with which acts of dishonesty occur. The worst offenders will still cheat, while those least likely to plagiarize an assignment still won't and may bristle at having to write a disclaimer on every paper and test. You can almost hear the students: "I still see people cheating all the time. Why are we doing this?"

The answer lies in the fairly slim margin of students whose conscience overcomes the temptation to cheat given a gentle nudge or those for whom a simple reminder may be enough to correct errors of process. Donald McCabe's research (summarized in an article titled "New Research on Academic Integrity" [College Administration Publications n.d.]) clearly demonstrates such improvements on college campuses (Figure 7.2).

Note that, according to McCabe's research, cheating and plagiarism are still committed at some point by almost *one-half* of all students. Still, the effects of an honor code at the institutional level are clear; honor codes tend to reduce academic dishonesty. That prevalence of cheating, too, means that students may not perceive honor codes as valuable, especially if they're not treated that way by faculty or schools.

In fact, I'd argue that an honor code works *only* if it's consistently and fairly implemented, subject to discussion, transparent, and open to revision.

> ## Voices from the Classroom
>
> It's amazing some of the kids who still put the honor pledge at the top of their papers. I never say it, I never emphasize it, but the eighth-grade teacher does. He makes them put their names, date, and the pledge, like a religious experience. I have enough trouble just getting them to remember their names on the paper. I think they're going to copy whether they put their name—it does nothing. Guilt does everything—I can lay that on thick. But the pledge doesn't hurt, either.
>
> —*Ninth-grade teacher*

| Serious Cheating on Campuses | | | |
|---|---|---|---|
| **When** | **Private Campuses with Honor Code** | **Large Public University with Modified Honor Code** | **Campuses with No Honor Code** |
| On tests | 23 percent | 33 percent | 45 percent |
| On written work | 45 percent | 50 percent | 56 percent |

*Figure 7.2*

## Teaching Opportunities

None of the suggestions that follow are likely to turn average students into little angels who rush home after school to memorize *The Chicago Manual of Style*, but they will help instill a sense that an honor code is an integral part of your school community.

- *An honor pledge for student papers.* The act of writing a pledge on every paper (example: "I pledge on my honor that this paper represents my own work.") might just be enough to tip a few students toward the side of academic integrity, or at least caution, but it also provides the basis for a discussion about integrity in school culture and for teachable moments about attribution. One teacher recently summed up his view of the honor pledge in his school nicely for me: "You can't make the horse drink the water," he said, "but you can hold his head under the surface and make him think about it good and hard."

- *Regular student-driven reminders and thoughts on the subject.* School assemblies, newspaper editorials, poster campaigns, and morning announcements can all serve as forums for the discussion of plagiarism *by* students *for* students. Students need to hear from their peers on such matters, not just from adults.

- *Advisory-style discussion.* Many schools now include faculty advisors—teachers and administrators who meet regularly with small groups of students to discuss matters of character education and civic agency, as well as school-related academic and behavioral issues. Plagiarism is a natural topic for such small meetings—removed from the regular classroom and academic performance, students may feel more free to speak their minds and listen to teachers and each other.

- *The honor code as a part of the curriculum.* Within academic courses, reference to a school's honor code on a regular basis demonstrates to students that teachers recognize and think about the guidelines as well. This practice cuts both ways, however; most honor codes include the expectation of student honesty, and teachers need to reflect that expectation in their own practice.

> ### Voices from the Classroom
>
> The honor code should become a main part of the curriculum; it sits in a book at many schools and it becomes very inorganic. Within course work, with advisors, the question should be asked as to how students see the honor code applying to certain situations. Certain pieces of literature really lend themselves to that discussion. Honor codes become stone monuments that aren't attended to, and that doesn't help anyone.
>
> —*School principal*

## YOU NEED TO KNOW: Traditional and Modified Honor Codes

The following definition comes from an interview with Donald McCabe reported by College Administration Publications (n.d.) and further clarifies his research about honor codes:

> Strong traditional academic honor codes often include such provisions as unproctored exams, the use of some form of pledge that students are asked to sign attesting to the integrity of their work, and a strong (often exclusive) student role in the judicial system that addresses allegations of academic dishonesty. Some traditional codes also include provisions that encourage or require students to report any cheating they may see among other students.
>
> Modified honor code approaches typically include a strong or exclusive role for students in the judicial process but generally do not mandate unproctored exams or the use of a pledge, although they can often be used at an instructor's option in selected courses. What modified honor code approaches do, however, is place a strong campus focus on the issue of academic integrity. I believe this simple fact alone explains much of the success of modified honor codes. Students are reminded, often quite frequently, that their campus places a high value on the question of academic integrity. Policies are clearly communicated to students, and they are asked to personally exercise responsibility for academic integrity.

Perceptions of fairness and transparency matter—honor codes fail if they *seem* biased or arbitrary, even if they aren't. "An effective honor code," write McCabe, Trevino, and Butterfield, "must be more than mere window dressing; a truly effective code must be well implemented and strongly embedded" (2001, 224). Faculty members need to discuss honor codes and the implementation of them with one another and administrators in formal and informal settings; they also need to be willing to modify and change codes as necessary. The basics of an honor code may have existed for one hundred years, but if the details have never changed to reflect Internet usage, for instance, students won't see it as a vital policy or part of their own culture.

## A Career in Modeling: How Teacher Attitudes and Discussion Influence Students

The students enrolled in my classes are so sick of talking about plagiarism that they probably wish I'd just copied the last chapter of this book from someone else. As I thought through aspects of plagiarism while writing the book, I regularly turned on a video camera and started asking them questions about assignments and honor codes and peer pressure. At the same time, I noticed an interesting shift in my classes—though they joked about it, those students now possessed a deeper understanding of academic integrity than any group I'd taught. Their internal rules may or may not have squared perfectly with mine, but they were thinking about it. "I double-checked all of my web links," a senior emailed me before turning in his assignment, "because I didn't want to call down the wrath of the plagiarism deities surrounding your room."

### My Classroom, My School

Each year my school holds an honor assembly, a gathering of all the students in our school auditorium. Students, not teachers, come to the stage to discuss aspects of the honor code and how they see them applying to real situations in the classroom. Then students are invited to sign an honor book that includes signatures of students collected over many years. The signing takes place behind a curtain, individually; students have the choice to sign or not to sign. Not signing the book does not release students from the honor code; rather, the choice to sign is presented as a possibility to make a personal commitment to integrity and honorable behavior.

In my own classroom, I don't require a pledge on student papers, though many teachers on campus do. Instead, I discuss citation and attribution before each and every major paper—both how to cite and *why*—and try to make the honor code work *for* students when possible. I sometimes trust the seniors I teach to take tests on their own, to make up in-class essays at home, or to bring their own notes into an exam. Do they cheat? Probably some do, but by discussing their practice, and what's right and wrong, *before* I make such assignments, I believe that I significantly cut down on cheating and plagiarism and build an expectation of maturity and professionalism that students respect.

Discussion of plagiarism and cheating with students works, and it needs to take place in two steps. First of all, it's worthwhile to discuss the culture of sharing in which adolescents operate. This culture begins, but doesn't end, with the Internet, where music, movies, and television shows are all available for the taking, often without clear-cut parameters of legality. But consider the world beyond the Internet. Teachers and other professionals photocopy articles and books regularly, even when it amounts to copyright infringement (the article you copy for your classes is legal, while the article you copy for the teacher next door isn't). Businesses heavily emphasize teamwork and journalists don't have to cite their sources, but neither condones plagiarism.

The result? Students sometimes look for ways to justify the choice to take the easy route in obtaining information or other intellectual products. In an article from the National Council of Teachers of English's *Council Chronicle*, professor Jeffrey R. Galin offers one way in which this occurs:

> Students have grown accustomed to downloading videos and music from the Internet and have even developed rationalizations such as "I can get this for free," or "This person has so much money, he or she won't miss a little more." (2005)

It doesn't hurt to inform students about the legalities of intellectual property (many of those I teach have no idea that they're breaking the law by downloading materials for free), but even without moralizing, discussions about the difficulties of navigating the Internet, and even our culture, ethically can be profitable.

The second line of discussion is a personal one. Students need to hear from adults not just rules and admonitions but accounts of the real dilemmas we face and how we solve them.

"Here's a question," I said to a group of about eight seniors one day. "I went to the grocery store with my three-year-old and spent about a hundred bucks. When I got back to the car, my daughter was crying about something, it was starting to rain, and I realized I hadn't paid for the bag of dog food on the bottom of my cart. Should I have gone back and paid, or driven home?"

Their answer: the store made the mistake, so it was their loss. My answer: I kept the bag in my car, and when I went back to the store a few days later, I put the bag in my cart and paid for it at the register along with my other groceries.

I have the same kinds of discussions with students about issues of academic integrity. I describe to students the terrible choices I made as a high school junior writing a research paper on the bombing of Hiroshima (the D+ was well deserved). I share tricky citation issues with them and discuss plagiarism in the news. Such discussions not only clear up misunderstandings about the definition of plagiarism but also elicit deeper thought about nuances and decision-making.

## Get Cut, or Cut and Paste? Other Factors in Plagiarism

Schools wishing to reduce incidences of plagiarism (and cheating in general) would do well to pay attention to the statistics that tell us about the tendencies of certain constituencies within the overall student population. A few examples follow.

### Males

#### THE ISSUE

When asked, "How many times have you copied an Internet document for a classroom assignment in the past year?" by the Josephson Institute (2006b) in a survey titled "The Ethics of America's Youth," 40 percent of high school boys answered that they had done so at least once, compared with 26 percent of girls (the numbers for middle school: 28 percent and 19 percent, respectively). Most studies, though not all, back up this inequity.

#### THE ANSWER

In the same survey, more boys than girls agreed with the statement, "Most adults in my life consistently set a good example of ethics and character." Around 50 percent of boys in middle and high school asserted the importance of being a person of "good character." Boys aren't a lost cause, even if what they believe about ethics and character doesn't always square with how they *act*—such is the nature of adolescents. Nor are girls so much more virtuous than boys that teachers can ignore one gender or the other in making policies. Teachers can, though, be aware of any particular aspects of peer pressure or other pressures created by the culture of their schools and consider gender in making decisions about group work and assignments. Sometimes encouraging students to talk about gender differences in terms of expectations and motivation reveals deeper issues about a class or school that can help a teacher understand where plagiarism comes from and how to prevent it.

### Athletes

#### THE ISSUE

The Josephson Institute's 2006 survey of high school athletes ("Are Coaches Teaching Our Young Athletes the Right Way to Play?") reveals that only slightly more high school athletes (66 percent compared with 60 percent) cheat in general than nonathletes, but the specifics are more

Discussion questions for faculty about the role of school culture are available online in the *Plagiarism Study Guide* at www.heinemann .com/gilmore.

alarming. For football players, the cheating rate rises to 72 percent (female swimmers are least likely to cheat). Forty-one percent of boys (and 25 percent of girls) think it's OK to use a stolen playbook. There's good news, though: 90 percent of athletes think coaches want them to do the right thing ethically "no matter what the cost."

### THE ANSWER

Involving coaches in discussions of academic dishonesty as well as dishonesty on the playing field is an obvious course of action for schools wishing to address plagiarism, and the connection between cheating in sports and cheating on school work resonates with many students. In addition, discussing time constraints with student athletes (and helping them find ways to resolve tensions created by those constraints) may help students balance their workload and practice schedule without resorting to plagiarism.

### *Underachievers and Top Achievers*

### THE ISSUE

It's been widely reported that a 1998 survey by *Who's Who Among American High School Students* found that 80 percent of the "best of the nation's 16- to 18-year olds" cheated to get there (Goode 1999). It's also true, however, that underachieving students are more likely to plagiarize and cheat than other students, or, as a 1999 Educational Testing Service fact sheet puts it, "Students with lower GPA's or those at the very top" are most likely to cheat.

### THE ANSWER

No school wants to create a school culture in which low-achieving students feel persecuted, less trusted than their peers, or held to different standards; the resentment that may stem from such perceptions is likely to lead to an increase in academic dishonesty. Nonetheless, one might consider the pressures the school puts on students at the bottom of the GPA (grade point average) scale as well as the pressure on those at the very top—the highest achievers—and work either to alleviate some of that pressure or to help students cope with it without resorting to academic dishonesty.

## The Bottom Line: School Culture Matters

Most writers about plagiarism conclude in a similar fashion, by calling for attention to the subject at the institutional level. It may not be original advice, but that's because, in the end, it just makes sense for academic institutions to unite on this issue. McCabe, Trevino, and Butterfield put it this way:

> Academic institutions are advised to consider ways of creating an "ethical community" on their campuses—one that includes clear communication of rules and standards, moral socialization of community members, and mutual respect between students and faculty. . . . Building an ethical community also might involve techniques such as creating a "hidden curriculum" in which students not only receive formal ethics instruction but also learn by actively discussing ethical issues and acting on them. (2001, 228)

I see no reason for this secondary curriculum to be hidden at all. Students should be aware that a discussion of ethics and rules is woven through the curriculum no matter the discipline. School culture is organic and, ideally, includes at least some aspects of democracy; without frank and open discussion and a willingness to involve students in rule making, schools can't develop community, only obedience.

There's a sort of irony embodied in this notion: preventing plagiarism demands a collaborative effort. Consequence without a sense of student ownership is really more akin to punishment, not learning. Focusing on detection reduces schools to an us versus them mentality that doesn't serve the needs of students to internalize and understand the difficult rules and expectations that surround them. Strict plagiarism policies don't encourage teachers to revisit assignments or classroom practice.

I began this book with a story about Helen Keller. One of the most important aspects of Keller's own account is that it is a self-reflection, written as an adult, of a difficult episode in her life. Keller's own vindication is, in some ways, the very eloquence of her later writing. But there's another aspect of the story that bears mentioning as well: the reaction of the adults surrounding the incident. Keller's teacher, Anne Sullivan, wrote at length about Keller's remarkable memory and described several pieces that Keller "plagiarized" in the same unintentional manner. Even

---

**Voices from the Classroom**

By tenth grade, if you've been caught and there was a specific consequence, you learn a lesson. Past that point, most students know right from wrong. The first inclination, though, is to think that the older students are, the more mature they are and the less likely to cheat or plagiarize. But the younger kids are actually less likely to cheat—they still respect authority; their ideas of right and wrong are black and white. Older students develop a sense of arbitrariness and ask themselves, "Well, is it really wrong?" But remember, our brains aren't really fully developed until we reach our twenties, so the decision-making process for a teen is *not* what an adult thinks it should be. Expectations and consequences still matter for just that reason.

—*School counselor*

more remarkable, I think, is the response of Margaret T. Canby, the author from whom Keller plagiarized (and whose work is now far eclipsed by Keller's own writings). Canby wrote to Anne Sullivan:

> What a wonderfully active and retentive mind that gifted child must have. . . . No one shall be allowed to think it was anything wrong; and some day she will write a great, beautiful story or poem that will make many people happy. Tell her there are a few bitter drops in every one's cup, and the only way is to take the bitter patiently, and the sweet thankfully. (Keller 1952, 344–45)

Keller benefited from the understanding and patience of adults; there were consequences for her mistake, but it was treated as a mistake, not a crime, nor a disease, nor a personal attack. Plagiarism doesn't always occur as a result of such innocence, but when committed by adolescents, it demands of teachers careful thought, judicious response, and, eventually, self-reflection.

I do not believe that plagiarism is a plague, but I do believe that the culture of learning—in a school, in a classroom, in a single student's expectations of himself—is the key to combating plagiarism, whether it happens as a mistake or a crime. Ultimately, we want students to love writing, to take joy in composition, even when it's hard work. We want them to value the process that adds their voices to those of others. That message is sent through our own modeling, through the society we create for students, and through imparting to students the skills to examine critically the culture that exists beyond the classroom.

## Works Cited

American Psychological Association (APA). 1998. "Research Shows Homework Does Boost Academic Achievement; but Overemphasizing Grades and Performance May Lead to Cheating." *ScienceDaily*, Mar. 4. www.sciencedaily.com/releases/1998/03/980304073520.htm (accessed Mar. 23, 2008).

*College Administration Publications*. n.d. "New Research on Academic Integrity: The Success of 'Modified' Honor Codes." www.collegepubs.com/ref/SFX000515.shtml (accessed Mar. 23, 2008).

Educational Testing Service. 1999. "Academic Cheating Fact Sheet." www.glass-castle.com/clients/www-nocheating-org/adcouncil/research/cheatingfactsheet.html (accessed Mar. 23, 2008).

Goode, Stephen. 1999. "Students Get A+ for Easy Cheating." *Insight on the News*. http://findarticles.com/p/articles/mi_m1571/is_35_15/ai_55927016 (accessed May 29, 2008).

James, Susan D. 2008. "Cheating Scandals Rock Three Top-Tier High Schools." ABC News. http://abcnews.go.com/US/story?id=4362510&page=1 (accessed Mar. 29, 2008).

The Josephson Institute. 2006. "Are Coaches Teaching Our Young Athletes the Right Way to Play?" http:// josephsoninstitute.org/sports/programs/survey/index.html (accessed Mar. 23, 2008).

———. 2006b. "The Ethics of American Youth." 2006. http://charactercounts .org/programs/reportcard/2006/data-tables.html (accessed Mar. 23, 2008).

Keller, Helen. 1952. *The Story of My Life*. Garden City, NY: Doubleday.

Kellogg, Alex P. 2002. "Students Plagiarize Less than Many Think, a New Study Finds." *Chronicle of Higher Education*. http://chronicle.com/free/2002/02/2002020101t.htm (accessed Mar. 23, 2008).

Kohn, Alfie. 2006. "The Trouble with Rubrics." *English Journal* 95: 12–15.

McCabe, Donald L., and Linda K. Trevino. 1997. "Individual and Contextual Influences on Academic Dishonesty: A Multicampus Investigation." *Research in Higher Education* 38: 379–96.

McCabe, Donald L., Linda K. Trevino, and Kenneth D. Butterfield. 2001. "Cheating in Academic Institutions: A Decade of Research." *Ethics and Behavior* 11: 219–31.

Nagelson, Sandra. 2007. "Academic Misconduct by University Students: Faculty Perceptions and Responses." *Plagiary: Cross-Disciplinary Studies in Plagiarism, Fabrication, and Falsification* 1: 1–10.

*National Council of Teachers of English*. 2005. *The Council Chronicle*. www.ncte.org/pubs/chron/highlights/122871.htm (accessed Feb. 18, 2008).

Wilson, Maja. 2006. *Rethinking Rubrics in Writing Assessment*. Portsmouth, NH: Heinemann.

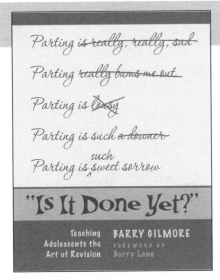
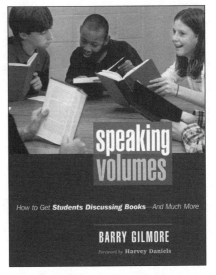